Leading Issues in Innovation Research Volume 2

Edited by Heather Fulford

Leading Issues in Innovation Research
Volume Two

Copyright © 2015 The authors
First published September 2015

All rights reserved. Except for the quotation of short passages for the purposes of critical review, no part of this publication may be reproduced in any material form (including photocopying or storing in any medium by electronic means and whether or not transiently or incidentally to some other use of this publication) without the written permission of the copyright holder except in accordance with the provisions of the Copyright Designs and Patents Act 1988, or under the terms of a licence issued by the Copyright Licensing Agency Ltd, Saffron House, 6-10 Kirby Street, London EC1N 8TS. Applications for the copyright holder's written permission to reproduce any part of this publication should be addressed to the publishers.

Disclaimer: While every effort has been made by the editor, authors and the publishers to ensure that all the material in this book is accurate and correct at the time of going to press, any error made by readers as a result of any of the material, formulae or other information in this book is the sole responsibility of the reader. Readers should be aware that the URLs quoted in the book may change or be damaged by malware between the time of publishing and accessing by readers.

Note to readers: Some papers have been written by authors who use the American form of spelling and some use the British. These two different approaches have been left unchanged.

ISBN: 978-1-910810-40-8 (print)
978-1-910810-41-5 (e-Pub)
978-1-910810-42-2 (Kindle)

Printed by Lightning Source POD

Published by: Academic Conferences and Publishing International Limited, Reading, RG4 9AY, United Kingdom, info@academic-publishing.org
Available from www.academic-bookshop.com

Contents

About the Editor ii

List of Contributing Authors iii

Introduction to Leading Issues in Innovation Research Volume 2
Heather Fulford vi

Innovation Performance, Innovation Capacity and Growth in Small Enterprises: an Enterprise-Level Analysis
Helena Forsman 1

Using Innovation to Stimulate Growth in Owner Managed SMEs
Paul Donaldson 21

Inter-Firm Alliances: A Mechanism to Develop Innovative Capacity in Portuguese SMEs
Luís Valentim, Mário Franco and João Lisboa 37

Service Innovation: A Smaller Firm Perspective
Edward McKeever, Sarah Jack and Danny Soetanto 53

Catalysts and Barriers of Open Innovation for SMEs in Transition Economy
Allan Lahi and Tiit Elenurm 71

Strategic Creativity as a Strength in Microsized Enterprises
Tiina Tarvainen 89

Analysis of the Relationship Between the Company's Internal Resources and the Effectiveness of Innovative Activity of SMEs in Poland
Tomasz Norek 105

About the Editor

Professor Heather Fulford is the Academic Director of the Centre for Entrepreneurship and Research Coordinator for the Department of Management at Aberdeen Business School, Robert Gordon University in Scotland. Her research interests include: innovation in SMEs, enterprise education, business start-up support and resources, and social enterprise. Heather delivers programmes on enterprise and employability, and new venture creation.

List of Contributing Authors

Paul Donaldson, Sysco, St Helens, UK

Tiit Elenurm, Estonian Business School, Tallinn, Estonia

Helena Forsman, The University of Winchester, UK

Mário Franco, University of Beira Interior, Covilhã, Portugal

Sarah Jack, Lancaster University Management School

Allan Lahi, Estonian Business School, Tallinn, Estonia

João Lisboa, University of Coimbra, Coimbra, Portugal

Edward McKeever, Lancaster University Management School

Tomasz Norek, University of Szczecin, Szczecin, Poland

Danny Soetanto, Lancaster University Management School

Tiina Tarvainen, University of Eastern Finland, Joensuu, Finland

Luís Valentim, University of Coimbra, Coimbra, Portugal

Introduction to Leading Issues in Innovation Research Volume 2

> *"Leading strategic thinkers are moving beyond the traditional product and service innovations to pioneering innovation in processes, value chains, business models, and all functions of management. Thus, innovative attitudes and behaviours are necessary for firms of all sizes to prosper and flourish in competitive environments"* (Kuratko, Goldsby and Hornsby 2012:4).

In my introduction to *Case Studies in Innovation Research: For Researchers, Teachers and Students* (2012), I noted that innovation is not an isolationist activity, but rather it is relational. In this volume of papers, which is devoted to research on innovation in Small and Medium-Sized Enterprises (SMES), that point about relationship and innovation emerges once more, and is reinforced by the findings of a number of the studies. A key issue for the management of an SME to contend with is knowing how to build relationships successfully in order to be able sustain innovative thinking and behaviour beyond the start-up phase of an enterprise. This requires the owner-manager or management team of an SME to look to their internal resources to identify innovative individuals among their workforce. An organisational culture or environment needs to be established in which those individuals are valued, can flourish and are empowered with the freedom to engage in innovative activity for the benefit of the enterprise as a whole. Fostering a culture of innovation like this requires strategic thinking on the part of management, and at times more formal planning, resource management and leadership than is typical in many smaller enterprises. The constraints of limited resource, whether time, money, or human capacity, can render this focus on planning, management and leadership considerably demanding for SMEs.

In addition, for many SMEs there is a need to look beyond their internal resources and capacity to stimulate or enhance their innovation activity. Partnerships and alliances need to be formed and nurtured with external agencies, including other players in the marketplace, larger enterprises, professional and trade associations, local and regional business networks, and knowledge-based organisations such as universities and research institutes. Successful development of such collaborations again requires careful and measured strategic thinking on the part of management. The benefits of collaborative working, and of participating in relevant networks, need to be acknowledged and understood; networking skills need to be honed; strategies must be formulated for accessing external resources efficiently and effectively; and approaches need to be developed for tapping into the knowledge and information available beyond organisational boundaries.

The papers selected for inclusion in this volume explore some of these issues relating to innovation stimulation and management in SMEs. The studies reported in these papers provide starting points for thought-provoking discussion and reflection on themes such as innovation and growth, innovation alliances, open innovation, and resource management for innovation. The papers raise questions about the role innovation plays in an SME's ability to be competitive and sustainable, as well as some broader questions about the contribution of small firm innovation in the wider growth and development of a nation, including in transition and developing economies. The research papers have been selected from papers published first in the refereed proceedings of the *European Conference on Innovation and Entrepreneurship* or the proceedings of the *International Conference on Innovation and Entrepreneurship*.

As Kuratko, Goldsby and Hornsby (2012:5) note, in the "constantly changing economic environment" of the twenty-first century, "innovative thinking has become a critical skill". The challenge for the entrepreneurs leading today's SMEs is to combine that innovative thinking with a careful process of innovation management, knowledge management and organisational learning.

References
Fulford, H. (2012) Case Studies in Innovation Research: For Researchers, Teachers and Students. Reading: Academic Publishing International.
Kuratko, D. F., Goldsby, M. G. and Hornsby, J. S. (2012) Innovation acceleration: transforming organisational thinking. New Jersey: Pearson Education, Inc.

Heather Fulford
Centre for Entrepreneurship
Aberdeen Business School

Innovation Performance, Innovation Capacity and Growth in Small Enterprises: an Enterprise-Level Analysis

Helena Forsman
The University of Winchester, Winchester Business School, UK
Originally published in The Proceedings of ECIE 2011

Editorial commentary

In this paper, Forsman wrestles with the relationship between business growth and innovation. This theme has been explored quote extensively elsewhere in the literature, and as Forsman notes, conflicting results have been obtained. In her study, Forsman adds a useful dimension to this topic by considering innovation capacity and innovation performance in the context of small enterprises.

The study is based on two datasets encompassing innovation performance and innovation capacity. Through statistical analysis of these datasets, Forsman establishes a clear link between innovation performance, innovation capacity and growth in small enterprises. In addition, her data provides insights into the characteristics of various kinds of innovator, including radical and incremental innovators. The innovation performer profiles presented in Table 3 in the paper could serve as a basis for further research in order to generate a deeper understanding of types of innovator in small enterprises and the specific characteristics of each type.

Some points for discussion, learning and reflection arising from this paper include:
- The role of innovation in small enterprise sustainability;
- How owner managers of small enterprises approach innovation or devise innovation strategies;
- The value of developing an innovation portfolio in small enterprises;
- The challenges of transforming a small enterprise from being "occasionally innovative" to "intrinsically innovative".

Helena Forsman

Abstract: The aim of this paper is to identify the factors that are associated with the innovation performance of small enterprises having fewer than 50 employees. The empirical evidence is based on two quantitative datasets describing innovation performance, innovation capacity and growth in small enterprises. The first dataset consists of the self-reported data of the innovation capacity and innovation performance of small enterprises. The second dataset covering the period of four years comprises the annual key figures of enterprises. After removing the cases with missing and extreme values, the total number of enterprises is 296. The descriptive statistics and non-parametric methods are used in the analysis. The results suggest that the age of the enterprise and the degree of innovation capacity is associated with innovation performance. The enterprises characterised by radical and diversified innovation development are younger than the non-innovators or the incremental innovators. As regards innovation capacity, the degree of capacity increases while the innovation performance profile shifts from the non-innovator characterised by low innovation performance towards the diversified innovator characterised by high innovation performance. Instead, the findings of this study reveal only a weak, statistically insignificant relationship between growth and innovation performance. In summary, this study provides two contributions to academic literature. First, it crystallises the relationship between innovation performance, innovation capacity and growth in small enterprises. Second, the results deepen the existing literature by providing a detailed view of the characteristics of different kinds of innovation performers. The paper recommends also some implications and provides ideas for future research.

Keywords: Innovation capacity; Growth; Performance; Small enterprises

1 Introduction

Innovation is often connected with improved business performance and growth leading to a common argument that enterprises which actively pursue innovation are more successful than those that do not innovate. However, in the context of small business, the previous studies have indicated mixed results. Some scholars have identified a strong positive relationship between innovation performance and business success while others have found no permanent differences between innovators and non-innovators. While prior literature provides a wide range of studies on the relationship between innovation and growth, relatively little work has been published on the relationship between innovation capacity and innovation performance in the context of small business.

Challenged by the above inferences, this paper aims at identifying the factors that are associated with the innovation performance of small enterprises. The main research question is: Are there differences in contextual factors, innovation capacity and in growth across the enterprises having different kinds of innovation performance profiles? The empirical evidence is based on two quantitative datasets describing innovation and growth in small enterprises with fewer than 50 employees. The first dataset consists of self-reported information on innovation and innovation activities in enterprises during four years (2005-2008). The second dataset consists of the values of annual growth indicators reported from 2005 to 2008. The total number of small enterprises included in the analysis is 296. The main analysis is based on descriptive statistics and non-parametric tests.

The structure of this paper is as follows. The next section introduces theoretical constructs and justifies the variables used in this study. Subsequently, the methods are presented providing the details of data collection and analysis followed by the findings. In the final section the results are discussed with the aim of answering the proposed research question, the conclusions are summarised and the implications for future research are provided.

2 Theoretical background

2.1 Innovation performance

Innovation performance has often been operationalised by the measures of rate or speed. The speed of innovation generation usually reflects how fast innovation projects are developed (Kessler and Chakrabarti, 1996) while the rate of innovation has been measured as the total number of innovations generated within a time interval (cf. Damanpour and Gopalakrishnan, 2001). Alegre and Chiva (2008) suggest that innovation performance consists of two different dimensions: innovation efficacy and innovation efficiency. Innovation efficacy reflects the degree of the success of an innovation and innovation efficiency indicates the efforts made to achieve that degree of success. The prior literature also suggests that the diversity of innovations is associated with performance and enterprises benefit from their capacity to be involved in the development of different innovation types (cf. Freel, 2000; Forsman and Temel 2011).

In this study, the innovation performance of enterprises is studied based on the approach which combines the constructs of innovation efficacy and the rate of innovation. The developed innovations which already have been exploited in business reflect innovation efficacy while the diversity of developed innovation types reflects the rate of innovation. For the identification of innovation performance, the developed innovations are separated to radical and incremental innovations (cf. Dewar and Dutton 1986). For the purpose of this study, an innovation is defined to be radical in nature if it differs dramatically from the competitors' concepts while it is defined to be incremental in nature if it is an improvement to an existing product, service, process or method (cf. Dewar and Dutton, 1986). Within the groups of radical and incremental, innovations are separated to product/service innovations and process/method innovations (cf. Forsman and Rantanen, 2011). The product/service innovation represents an innovation type that is visible to external stakeholders, such as customers. Correspondingly, the process/method innovation represents an innovation type which can be the result of internal development, and it is not necessarily visible to outsiders. This combined grouping was selected because the distinction between different innovation types is not always clear in small enterprises.

2.2 Growth

The existing literature introduces conflicting results of the relationship between growth and innovation. Some scholars have identified a strong positive link between innovation and growth while others have found no permanent differences between innovators and non-innovators (cf. Geroski and Machin, 1992; Roper, 1997). Freel (2000), who found that among the fast-growing category, innovators had better performance than non-innovators, suggests that growth should be studied through a clearer classification, e.g. among enterprises grouped into declining, stable, growth and super-growth enterprises.

The growth of an enterprise has often been operationalised by the measures of growth in sales, growth in profits and growth in productivity. Profitability has been measured by using profit margin, absolute profits and profits per employee while sales per employee has been used as a measure of productivity reflecting the internal efficiency of an enterprise (Freel, 2000; Heunks 1998; Verhees et al., 2010).

In this study growth will be examined by using two variables: the growth rate of annual sales (SALES) and profitability in terms of the rate of return on investment (ROI). The preliminary analysis revealed that productivity in terms of sales per employee is strongly associated with annual sales. On the other hand, profitability reflects also how efficiently an enterprise uses its resources. On the premise of the above, productivity in terms of sales per employee was excluded from the analysis. As suggested by Freel (2000), growth will be examined by using classification which separates declining and growing enterprises.

2.3 Innovation capacity

The capacity to innovate has been widely studied as a predictor of innovation performance, but there is no common definition to innovation capacity. Szeto (2000) defines innovation capacity as a continuous improvement of capabilities and resources that an enterprise possesses to explore and exploit new business opportunities. Amit and Schoemaker (1993) distinguish resources from capabilities by stating that resources are stocks of available factors that are owned or controlled by an organisation. Capabilities, on the other hand, refer to the capacity to deploy the resources of an organisation.

As regards resources, formal RD efforts have been viewed in literature as an indicator of the internal resources of innovation development. However, innovation often involves informal RD activities such as experimentation, learning, evaluation and the adaptation of technologies (Santamaría et al., 2009). This could result in difficulties in distinguishing innovation development from other business activities, especially in small enterprises in which the development work is integrated into their daily activities (Forsman 2008). In order to increase the resources, several scholars have suggested that enterprises should participate in collaborative networks (e.g. Caniëls and Romijn, 2003). Opportunities to improve knowledge, access to external resources and lower RD costs have been introduced as the main advantages of networking (e.g. Karaev et al., 2007).

Capabilities have been introduced as a transforming ability between resources and innovation goals (Amit and Schoemaker, 1993). It is a well-established empirical fact that the accumulation of existing knowledge plays an important role in innovation. With a low level of existing knowledge, an enterprise is not able to internalise and exploit the external knowledge. Absorptive capacity is a commonly used concept to describe the ability of an enterprise to recognise the value of new external knowledge, to assimilate it and to apply it to commercial ends (Cohen and Levinthal, 1990). In accordance with the concept of absorptive capacity, Teece (2007) defines that the dynamic capabilities of an enterprise consist of sensing and shaping new opportunities, seizing opportunities, and orchestrating and reconfiguring the intangible and tangible assets of the enterprise for maintaining its competitiveness (see also Branzei and Vertinsky, 2006).

In addition to the dynamic capabilities, literature provides a variety of research results about the capabilities that are needed to develop a certain particular type of innovation. The importance of customer orientation and market knowledge have been emphasised for developing product innovations (Hernandez-Espallardo and Delgado-Ballester, 2009) as well as for generating radical innovations. Danneels (2002) highlights the importance of a proactive approach which requires building an understanding of the needs of customers that are as yet unidentified. Herrmann et al. (2007) add to this that risk-propensity is essential for developing radical innovations. Finally, some researchers have found that the development of radical innovations demands the disruption of existing capabilities while incremental innovation development requires the enhancements of existing capabilities (e.g. Ellonen et al., 2009; Forsman and Annala, 2011).

On the basis of the above, this paper explores innovation capacity based on three types of variables: the rate of RD investments indicating the degree of internal resources, benefits gained through networking reflecting the degree of external resources and finally, the degree of capabilities demonstrating the ability of an enterprise to utilise its internal and external resources.

2.4 Contextual factors

One common contextual factor used in prior literature is the age of an enterprise. It has been suggested that enterprise maturity affects innovation development through increased structural inertia (cf. Freel 2005). Along with age, Hernández-Espallardo and Delgado-Ballester (2009) pay attention to the influence of the industrial sector on innovation development. Innovation development within manufacturing enterprises has been studied with emphasis on the technology intensity of sectors while within service enterprises the focus has been on the knowledge intensity of sectors (Amara et al., 2009; Forsman, 2011; Pavitt, 1984).

On the premise of the above, the age of the enterprise and the knowledge and technology intensity of the industrial sector of the enterprise are used as contextual variables.

3 Methodology

The aim of this paper is to identify the factors that are associated with the innovation performance of small enterprises having fewer than 50 employees. The main research question is: Are there differences in growth, innovation capacity and in contextual factors across the enterprises characterised by the different kinds of innovation performance profiles? The null hypothesis is that there are no differences and it is rejected at the level of significance $p \leq .05$.

3.1 Data and methods

The empirical evidence is based on two quantitative datasets describing innovation performance, innovation capacity and growth in small enterprises. The first dataset, which was gathered in January 2009, consists of the self-reported data of the innovation capacity and innovation performance of small enterprises. The second dataset covering the period of four years from 2005 to 2008 comprises the annual key figures of enterprises. After removing the cases with missing and extreme values, the total number of enterprises is 296.

In the main analysis, the descriptive statistics are used to examine the general patterns of innovation performance. Because the data exhibits skewness, which implies departures from normality, the distribution-free nonparametric tests were considered to be a suitable statistical technique for analysing the data of this study. The Kruskal-Wallis test is used for unrelated multi-group comparisons to test whether there exist statistically significant differences across the innovation performance profiles. The Mann-Whitney post hoc test is used for two-group comparisons to test where exactly the differences lie.

In order to avoid inflated error rates, a Bonferroni correction is applied in post-hoc tests to adjust a more stringent critical value of significance (Field, 2009). The new value of significance is calculated by dividing the used level (Sig. $\leq .05$) by the number of post hoc tests. The effect size is calculated by converting the Z-score into the effect size estimate r:

$$r = \frac{Z}{\sqrt{N}}$$

3.2 Variables

3.2.1 Innovation performance

An innovation performance profile was specified for every enterprise based on the responses to the question of what are the innovation types that have been developed in enterprises during the past four years. The profile was identified based on the radicalness of developed innovations and the diversity of developed innovation types.

Four profiles arose from the data: a non-innovator, an incremental innovator, a radical innovator and a diversified innovator. The non-innovators consist of the enterprises which have not developed any innovations during the past four years. The incremental innovators are enterprises in which innovation development is characterised exclusively by incremental improvements and the diversity of developed innovation types is low. Correspondingly, the radical innovators are enterprises which have developed also radical innovations but the diversity of developed innovation types is low. Finally, the fourth profile, the diversified innovators consists of the enterprises which have developed both radical and incremental innovations and in which the diversity of developed innovation types is high.

Classification analysis was used to observe whether enterprises were categorised as predicted. Based on it, the classification works quite well for each category. According to the results, 94.7% of the categorised respondents are correctly classified. Within the profile categories, 100.0% of the non-innovators, 90.6% of the incremental innovators, 96.4% of the radical innovators and 100.0% of the diversified innovators are classified as predicted.

3.2.2 Growth

Growth is studied based on two variables: growth in annual sales and growth in ROI. Regarding both variables, the data has been divided into three grower categories: 1) Decliners consisting of enterprises characterised by the lowest growth (25% of data), 2) Low growers comprising enterprises characterised by a low growth (50% of data) and finally, 3) High growers i.e. enterprises characterised by the highest growth (25% of data). Growth in sales and growth in ROI have been analysed separately.

3.2.3 Innovation capacity

Innovation capacity is examined by using three types of variables: the rate of RD investments indicating the degree of internal resources, benefits gained through networking reflecting the degree of external resources and finally, the degree of capabilities demonstrating the ability of an enterprise to utilise its internal and external resources.

The first variable of innovation capacity, the rate of RD investments, was reported by respondents in terms of the percentage of sales that had been invested in development activities. The responses have been coded into three groups: 1=<1%, 2=1-5% and 3=>5%.

The second variable, external input into innovation development through networking is studied based on three questions. The respondents assessed what impact networking had had on their business. The responses are graded by one (1) indicating benefits gained through networking, by zero (0) demonstrating no benefits related to the item in question and by minus one (-1) indicating disadvantages as a result of networking. The factor analysis using principal component approach with varimax rotation reveals the presence of one factor that accounts for 64.1% of the total variance. The Kaiser-Meyer-Olkin measure of sampling adequacy is .68 exceeding the recommended value of .60 (Jokivuori and Hietala, 2007). The internal consistency was measured with Cronbach's Alpha giving a value of .72. Also it is above the critical limit of 0.6 (Jokivuori and Hietala, 2007).

Based on the existing literature on innovation capabilities, 10 capability items are included in the analysis. The degree of the capabilities was reported based on a three-point scale: 1=low, 2=moderate and 3=high. The factor analysis using principal component approach with varimax rotation reveals the presence of three factors that accounts for 53.2% of the total variance: entrepreneurial capabilities, customer and market knowledge and finally, risk management capabilities. The Kaiser-Meyer-Olkin measure of sampling adequacy is .860. The internal consistency was measured with Cronbach's Alpha resulting values between .67 and .78. The items of each innovation capacity variable are reported in Table 1.

Helena Forsman

Table 1: The list of variables

Variables	Min	Max	
Innovation performance profile	1	4	
Growth			
Growth in annual sales	1	3	
Growth in ROI	1	3	
Resources			
Internal resources			
RD Investments	1	3	
External resources gained through networking	-1	1	Cronbach 's Alpha =.672
Input in innovation development			
External resources			
Acquired special knowledge			
Capabilities			
Entrepreneurial capabilities	-1	1	Cronbach 's Alpha =.777
Capabilities to recognise new opportunities			
Abilities to exploit external knowledge			
Capabilities to develop innovations			
Capabilities to create new business			
Market and customer knowledge	-1	1	Cronbach 's Alpha =.702
Capabilities to find new customers			
Abilities to expand to new markets			
Capabilities to increase sales to existing customers			
Risk management capabilities	-1	1	Cronbach 's Alpha =.732
Capabilities to risk assessment			
Willingness to risk taking			
Abilities to risk taking			
Contextual variables			
Age	1	4	
Knowledge-technology of industrial sector	1	4	

3.2.4 Contextual variables

Two contextual variables are included in the analysis: the age of the enterprise and the knowledge-technology intensity of the industrial sector of the enterprise. The age of the enterprise is categorised into four groups: 1=< 7 years since foundatios, 2=8-14 years, 3=15-21 years and 4=>21 years since foundation. The knowledge-technology intensity of the industrial sector has been identified following the taxonomy introduced by Pavitt (1984). The manufacturing enterprises have been grouped into four categories: 1=supplier dominated sectors (SD) characterised by relatively low knowledge-tech intensity, 2= scale intensive sectors (SI) representing medium knowledge-tech intensity and 3=specialised suppliers (SS) and 4=science based sectors (SB) characterised by high knowledge-tech intensity.

Based on Pavitt's (1984) taxonomy, Miozzo and Soete (2001) have modified an application to the service industries. This study uses it as a basis for grouping service enterprises into four categories: 1=supplier dominated sectors (SDS) characterised by low knowledge-tech intensity, 2=the sectors of scale intensive physical networks (PN) representing medium knowledge-tech intensity and 3=the sectors of scale intensive information networks (IN) and 4=specialised supplier sectors (SSS) characterised by high knowledge-intensity (see also Forsman, 2011). The coding principles follow the classification used by Castaldi (2009). Table 1 summarises the variables used in this study.

4 Findings

Table 2 presents the mean values and the significance values of the Kruskall Wallis Test for the variables. In general, it can be noticed that there are statistically significant differences in innovation capacity and in contextual variables across the innovation performance profiles. As regards growth, the findings demonstrate that the radical innovators and the diversified innovators have slightly higher values in annual sales growth than the other innovation performance profiles. In addition, the diversified innovators have the highest growth terms of ROI. Correspondingly, the incremental innovators have the lowest values in both, growth in sales and growth in profitability. Nevertheless, the results of the Kruskal Wallis Tests indicate that these differences are statistically insignificant (Sig.>.05).

The middle part of Table 2 presents the results for the variables of innovation capacity. The general figure is that the degree of innovation capacity increases while the innovation performance profile shifts from a non-innovator towards a diversified innovator. The results of the Kruskal Wallis Tests demonstrate that these differences are statistically significant regarding all innovation capacity variables ($.000 \leq p \leq .002$).

Six post hoc tests were carried out. The Bonferroni correction was applied and the new value of significance was $Sig. \leq .008$. The results of the post hoc tests demonstrate that the entrepreneurial capabilities of non-innovators are significantly lower with a small effect size than the capabilities of incremental innovators ($Z=-3.350$, $p=.001$, $r=-.25$). Further, the non-innovators have reported that their internal resources ($Z=-4.025$, $p=.000$, $r=-.43$), entrepreneurial capabilities ($Z=-5.620$, $p=.000$, $r=-.60$) and their risk management capabilities ($Z=-3.228$, $p=.001$, $r=-.34$) are significantly lower than the radical innovators have. As the above results demonstrate, the effect size is medium.

The relationship between incremental innovators and radical innovators is similar. Incremental innovators have reported that their internal resources ($Z=-3.399$, $p=.001$, $r=-.24$), entrepreneurial capabilities ($Z=-4.682$, $p=.000$, $r=-.33$) and their risk management capabilities ($Z=-3.617$, $p=.000$, $r=-.26$) are significantly lower than the values of radical innovators. The effect size is small to medium.

The differences are the largest between the diversified innovators and the non-innovators. The diversified innovators have reported that their innovation capacity is at a significantly higher level than that of the non-innovators. This finding is consistent regarding all innovation capacity items. The results of the Mann-Whitney Tests are: Internal resources ($Z=-5.618$, $p=.000$, $r=-.57$), external resources ($Z=-3.311$, $p=.001$, $r=-.33$), entrepreneurial capabilities ($Z=-5.056$, $p=.000$, $r=-.51$), market and customer knowledge ($Z=-2.650$, $p=.008$, $r=-.27$) and for risk management capabilities ($Z=-3.127$, $p=.002$, $r=-.32$). As the above results indicate, the effect size varies between small and medium.

There are also noticeable differences in all innovation capacity items between the diversified innovators and the incremental innovators. The results of the Mann-Whitney Tests for these differences are: Internal resources (Z=-6.190, p=.000, r=-.43), external resources (Z=-3.016, p=.003, r=-.21), entrepreneurial capabilities (Z=-3.948, p=.000, r=-.27), market and customer knowledge (Z=-3.108, p=.002, r=-.22) and for risk management capabilities (Z=-3.543, p=.000, r=-.25). The effect size is small to medium.

Regarding contextual variables, it can be noticed that the age of the enterprise decreases while the innovation performance profile shifts from the non-innovator towards the diversified innovator. On the contrary, knowledge-technology intensity increases when the profile moves from the non-innovator towards the diversified innovator. The four Mann-Whitney Post hoc tests were conducted to locate the differences. The Bonferroni correction was applied and the new value of significance was Sig.≤.013.

The results of post hoc tests indicate that the age of non-innovators is significantly higher with a small effect size than the age of radical innovators (Z=-2.748, Sig.=.006, r=-.29). The age of non-innovators is also significantly higher than the age of diversified innovators (Z=-2.786, Sig.=.005, r=-.28). As regards the knowledge-technology intensity of the industrial sector of enterprise, the six Mann-Whitney post hoc tests with a Bonferroni correction indicate that the differences across the innovation performance profiles are statistically insignificant (.014≤p≤.150).

In summary, when examining the differences across the innovation performance profiles, it can be found that the age of the enterprise and the degree of innovation capacity are associated with the profile. The enterprises characterised by radical and diversified innovation development are younger than the non-innovators or the incremental innovators. As regards innovation capacity, the non-innovators and the incremental innovators have reported about a significantly lower innovation capacity than the radical and diversified innovators. Instead, the results suggest that growth is not associated with innovation performance.

Table 2: The mean values of variables by innovator profile

	Non-innovator		Incremental innovator		Radical innovator		Diversified innovator		Kruskal Wallis Sig.
	Mean	Std	Mean	Std	Mean	Std	Mean	Std	
Growth profile									
Annual sales	2.00	.54	1.95	.73	2.06	.74	2.06	.72	.678
ROI	2.03	.75	1.95	.67	1.91	.71	2.17	.75	.139
Innovation Capacity									
Resources									
Internal resources	1.26	.56	1.49	.54	1.89	.77	2.14	.69	.000***
External resources	.74	.70	.93	.74	1.15	.81	1.27	.72	.002**
Capabilities									
Entrepreneurial capabilities	.37	.65	.84	.77	1.44	.74	1.33	.84	.000***
Customer and market knowledge	.69	.87	.78	.73	1.09	.81	1.14	.76	.002**
Risk management capabilities	.51	.66	.63	.71	1.09	.83	1.06	.84	.000***
Contextual variables									
Age	3.17	.75	2.96	.94	2.59	.96	2.60	.99	.004**
Knowledge-tech intensity	2.00	1.24	2.23	1.07	2.48	1.11	2.59	1.12	.028*
N	35		144		54		63		

5 Discussion and conclusions

The aim of this paper was to identify the factors that are associated with innovation performance in small enterprises. The main research question was: Are there differences in growth, innovation capacity and in contextual factors across the innovation performance profiles?

Table 3 summarises the characteristics of different innovation performance profiles. The most salient findings is that innovation performance is associated with innovation capacity. Instead, the findings of this study reveal only a weak, statistically insignificant relationship between growth and innovation performance. The findings indicate that the characteristics of non-innovators and incremental innovators are quite similar. Correspondingly, there exist several similarities between the radical innovators and the diversified innovators.

In line with prior literature (e.g. Szeto 2000: Forsman and Annala, 2011), the results suggest that the degree of innovation capacity increases while the innovation performance profile shifts from the non-innovator characterised by low innovation performance towards the diversified innovator characterised by high innovation performance. It seems that enterprises benefit from their capacity to be involved in the development of different innovation types (cf. Freel, 2000; Freeman, 1994). In line with Alegre and Chiva (2008), the results indicate that innovation capacity, and especially capabilities accumulate through learning along the innovation process. The capabilities of non-innovators and incremental innovators are at a lower level than the capabilities of the enterprises which have developed radical innovations i.e. radical and diversified innovators. This result is in line with prior studies suggesting that the development of radical innovations demands disruption of existing capabilities while the development of incremental innovations requires enhancements of existing capabilities (cf. Ellonen et al. 2009).

As Table 3 displays, the mean age of non-innovators is higher than it is in other profiles and their knowledge-technology intensity is low. This finding gives support to the research results which suggest that enterprise maturity affects innovation development through increased structural inertia (cf. Freel 2005). In addition, the non-innovators are characterised by low or very low innovation capacity. Nevertheless, these enterprises have had moderate growth in annual sales as well as in ROI. The characteristics of incremental innovators are similar. Their innovation capacity is at a low level, the mean age of these enterprises is quite high and the knowledge-technology intensity is at a moderate level. In addition, growth in sales and growth in ROI are both at a low level. According to Pavitt (1984), these enterprises are characterized by weak in-house RD and engineering capabilities. They adopt externally-acquired technology and make it function in a new environment (see also Hansen and Serin, 1997).

The characteristics of radical innovators differ from the above description. The enterprises of this profile are characterised by relatively high innovation capacity, the mean age of this profile is low and knowledge-technology intensity is high. The growth in sales is at a moderate level while the growth in ROI is at a low level. Davidsson et al. (2009) warn that the enterprises which pursue high sales growth starting from low profitability are not able to finance strategies towards building hard-to-copy competitive advantages. Following this reasoning, there is a risk that the radical innovators that pursue growth with low profitability will soon transit to below the average on both growth in sales and growth in profits.

The characteristics of diversified innovators have several similarities with radical innovators. Their innovation capacity is at a high or very high level, the mean age of the diversified innovators is low and their knowledge-technology intensity is at a high level. However, the value of annual sales growth is moderate while the value of growth in ROI is high. According to Davidsson et al. (2009), these enterprises are in a better position for achieving sustainable growth.

Table 3: Summary of the characteristics of the innovation performer profiles

	Non-innovator	Incremental innovator	Radical innovator	Diversified innovator
Growth profile				
Annual sales	Moderate	Low	Moderate	Moderate
ROI	Moderate	Low	Low	High
Innovation Capacity				
Resources				
Internal resources	Very low*	Low*	High*	Very high*
External resources	Low*	Low*	Moderate	High*
Capabilities				
Entrepreneurial capabilities	Very low*	Low*	High*	High*
Customer and market knowledge	Low*	Low*	High	High*
Risk management capabilities	Low*	Low*	High*	High*
Contextual variables				
Age	High*	Moderate	Low*	Low*
Knowledge-tech intensity	Low	Moderate	Moderate	High

Note: The levels in comparison to the mean scores of the variables, * supported by statistically significant differences

The findings also indicate that non-innovators and incremental innovators have reported less frequently about the advantages acquired through networking. Correspondingly, radical innovators and diversified innovators have gained networking benefits. Rosenbusch et al. (2011) found that internal innovation projects increase the performance of an enterprise substantially while innovation projects that involve external collaborators have no significant effect on performance. The results of this study give support to the above finding only regarding radical innovators.

In summary, this study provides two contributions to academic literature. First, it crystallises the relationship between innovation performance, innovation capacity and growth in small enterprises. Second, the results deepen the existing literature by providing a detailed view of the characteristics of the different kinds of innovators. The paper recommends also some implications. At an enterprise level, the results may help small business owner-managers to consider what might be the optimal innovation capacity for achieving the targeted level of innovation performance. At a public policy level, the results of this study give ideas for improving the innovation performance of small enterprises. Based on the results of this study, it can be recommended that attention should be paid to the diversity of innovations. It seems that in a longer run, the enterprises characterised by a flow of innovations have better innovation performance than those characterised by low diversity. This means that outputs of certain types of innovations may become the inputs of other innovation types (cf. Amara et al., 2009). In line with Geroski and Machin (1992), the above results also suggest that, in order to improve performance, small enterprises should be intrinsically innovative rather than occasionally innovative. Finally, the analysis of this study did not reveal any statistically significant relationship between growth and innovation performance. Tidd (2001) provides one potential explanation for this by stating that the relationship between innovation inputs and outputs is much weaker at an enterprise-level than it is at an industry-level. The analysis in this study has been carried out at an enterprise-level. It would be interesting to extend the analysis to industrial-level.

References

Alegre, J. and Chiva, R. (2008) "Assessing the Impact of Organizational Learning Capability on Product Innovation Performance: An Empirical Test", *Technovation*, Vol. 28, No. 6, pp. 315–326.

Amara, N. Landry, R. and Doloreux, D. (2009) "Patterns of Innovation in Knowledge-Intensive Business Services", *The Service Industries Journal*, Vol. 29, No. 4, pp. 407-430.

Amit, R. and Schoemaker, P.J.H. (1993) "Strategic Assets and Organizational Rent", *Strategic Management Journal*, Vol. 14, No. 1, pp. 33–46.

Branzei, O. and Vertinsky, I. (2006) "Strategic Pathways to Product Innovation Capabilities in SMEs", *Journal of Business Venturing*, Vol. 21, No. 1, pp. 75-105.

Caniëls, M.C.J. and Romijn, H.A. (2003) "SME Clusters, Acquisition of Technological Capabilities and Development: Concepts, Practice and Policy Lessons", *Journal of Industry, Competition and Trade*, Vol. 3, No. 3, pp. 187-210.

Castaldi, C. (2009) "The Relative Weight of Manufacturing and Services in Europe: an Innovation Perspective", *Technological Forecasting and Social Change*, Vol. 76, No. 6, pp. 709-722.

Cohen, W.M. and Levinthal, D.A. (1990) "Absorptive Capacity: a New Perspective on Learning and Innovation", *Administrative Science Quarterly*, Vol. 35, No. 1, pp. 128–152.

Damanpour, F. and Gopalakrishnan, S. (2001) "The Dynamics of the Adoption of Product and Process Innovations in Organizations", *Journal of Management Studies*, Vol. 38, No. 1, pp. 45–65.

Danneels, E. (2002) "The Dynamics of Product Innovation and Firm Competencies", *Strategic Management Journal*, Vol. 23, No. 12, pp. 1095-1121.

Dewar, R.D. and Dutton, J.E. (1986) "The Adoption of Radical and Incremental Innovations: an Empirical Analysis", *Management Science*, Vol. 32, No. 1, pp. 1422–1433.

Ellonen, H-K., Wikström, P. and Jantunen, A. (2009) "Linking Dynamic-Capability Portfolios and Innovation Outcomes", *Technovation*, Vol. 29, No. 11, pp. 753-762.

Field, A (2009) *Discovering Statistics Using SPSS*. 3rd Edition. London: SAGE Publications.

Forsman, H. (2008) "Business Development Success in SMEs. A Case Study Approach", *Journal of Small Business and Enterprise Development*, Vol. 15, No. 3, pp. 606–622.

Forsman, H. (2011) "Innovation Capacity and Innovation Development in Small Enterprises. A Comparison between the Manufacturing and Service Sectors", *Research Policy*, Vol. 40, No. 5, pp. 739-750.

Forsman, H. and Annala, U. (2011) "Small Enterprises as Innovators: Shift from a Low Performer to a High Performer", *International Journal of Technology Management*, Vol. 56, No. 1/2, (Forthcoming).

Forsman, H. and Rantanen, H. (2011) "Small Manufacturing and Service Enterprises as Innovators. A Comparison by Size", *European Journal of Innovation Management*, Vol.14, No. 1, pp. 27-50.

Freel, M.S. (2000) "Do Small Innovating Firms Outperform Non-Innovators?", *Small Business Economics*, Vol. 14, No. 3, pp. 195–210.

Freel, M.S (2005) "The Characteristics of Innovation-Intensive Small Firms: Evidence from Northern Britain", *International Journal of Innovation Management*, Vol. 9, No. 4, pp. 401-429.

Geroski, P and Machin, S. (1992) "Do Innovating Firms Outperform Non-Innovators?", *Business Strategy Review*, Vol. 3, No. 2, pp. 79–90.

Leading Issues in Innovation Research

Hansen, P., Serin, G. (1997) "Will low technology products disappear? The hidden innovation processes in low technology industries", *Technological Forecasting and Social Change*, Vol. 55, No. 2, pp. 179–191.

Hernández-Espallardo, M. and Delgado-Ballester, E. (2009) "Product Innovation in Small Manufacturers, Market Orientation and the Industry's Five Competitive Forces: Empirical Evidence from Spain", *European Journal of Innovation Management*, Vol. 12, No. 4, pp. 470-491.

Herrmann, A., Gassmann, O. and Eisert, U. (2007) "An Empirical Study of the Antecedents for Radical Product Innovations and Capabilities for Transformation", *Journal of Engineering and Technology Management*, Vol. 24, No. 1-2, pp. 92–120.

Heunks, F.J. (1998) "Innovation, Creativity and Success", *Small Business Economics*, Vol. 10, No. 3, pp. 263-272.

Jokivuori, P. and Hietala, R. (2007) *Määrällisiä tarinoita. Monimuuttujamenetelmien käyttö ja tulkinta.* WSOY, Helsinki.

Karaev, A., Koh, S.C.L. and Szamosi, L.T. (2007) "The Cluster Approach and SME Competitiveness: a Review", *Journal of Manufacturing Technology Management*, Vol. 18, No. 7, pp. 818–835.

Leiponen, A. (2005) "Organization of Knowledge and Innovation: the Case of Finnish Business Services", *Industry and Innovation*, Vol. 12, No. 2, pp. 185-203.

Miozzo, M. and Soete, L. (2001) "Internationalization of Services: a Technological Perspective", *Technological Forecasting and Social Science*, Vol. 67, No. 2/3, pp. 159-185.

Pavitt, K. (1984) "Sectoral Patterns of Technical Change: Towards a Taxonomy and a Theory", *Research Policy*, Vol. 13, No. 6, pp. 343-373.

Roper, S. (1997) "Product Innovation and Small Business Growth: a Comparison of the Strategies of German, UK and Irish Companies", *Small Business Economics*, Vol. 9, No. 6, pp. 523-537.

Rosenbusch, N., Brinckmann, J. and Bausch, A. (2011) "Is innovation always beneficial? A meta-analysis of the relationship between innovation and performance in SMEs", *Journal of Business Venturing*, Vol. 26, No. 4, pp. 441-457.

Santamaría, L., Nieto, M.J. and Barge-Gil, A. (2009) "Beyond Formal R&D: Taking Advantage of Other Sources of Innovation in Low- and Medium-Technology Industries", *Research Policy*, Vol. 38, No. 3, pp. 507-517.

Szeto, E. (2000) "Innovation Capacity: Working Towards a Mechanism for Improving Innovation within an Inter-Organizational Network", *The TQM Magazine*, Vol. 12, No. 2, pp. 149–158.

Teece, D.J. (2007) "Explicating Dynamic Capabilities: the Nature and Microfoundations of (Sustainable) Enterprise Performance", *Strategic Management Journal*, Vol. 28, No. 13, pp. 1319-1350.

Tidd, J. (2001) "Innovation Management in Context: Environment, Organization and Performance", International Journal of Management Reviews, Vol. 3, No. 3, pp. 169-183.

Verhees, F., Meulenberg, M. and Pennings, J. (2010) "Performance Expectations of Small Firms Considering Radical Product Innovation", *Journal of Business Research*, Vol. 63, No. 7, pp. 772-777.

Helena Forsman

Using Innovation to Stimulate Growth in Owner Managed SMEs

Paul Donaldson
Sysco, St Helens, UK
Originally published in The Proceedings of ICIE 2014

Editorial commentary

Donaldson draws on his experience as a consultant to large firms to investigate the role of innovation in stimulating the growth of SMEs. By observing entrepreneurial and strategic practice in SMEs, Donaldson challenges aspects of established theory. He is particularly interested in the role played by the owner-manager in leading the growth and development of an enterprise. Donaldson's study uses Soft Systems Methodology (SSM), and is focused on established owner-managed SMEs based in one region of England. He explores the way owner-mangers react to triggers, for example by moderating goals in times of threat, or pursuing innovation for growth in a time of perceived opportunity.

Some points for discussion, learning and reflection arising from this paper include:

- The characteristics of an innovation-oriented owner-manager.
- The role of the owner-manager in fostering innovation and growth in an SME.
- The possible perils of reliance on owner-manager to lead innovation.
- Owner-manager led innovation and succession planning in SMEs.

Abstract: This author has been involved in a considerable amount of consultancies and interventions in a large number of different organisations in the past 25 years. As a classically trained consultant, originally from the large firm sector, a dissonance was detected between advocated theory and observed practice, especially in the owner-manager sector which prompted this study. The research described in this paper was premised on the observation that modern economies rely on the growth of the small business sector, thus supporting this growth is a major economic concern for individual countries. The implicit view taken is that innovation underpins growth. This work was an action research project where the author conducted an inductive phenomological study using systems ideas as epistemological learning devices to advance knowledge. A set of intervention methods and principles have been developed to assist organisations to use innovation to determine and implement actions to achieve their chosen objectives at given points in time. The types of owner-managed small firms researched had all passed the two major SME barriers (see Daly et al, 1991 and Dunn and Bradstreet, 2001) of being in existence for more than 5 years, and development from micro to small firms. The literature suggests that the concept of growth in small firms is a significant and contentious issue, and questions the validity of the formal application of strategic theory to achieve growth in this specific context. The empirical research conducted in this work suggests that growth is not a planned process that emanates from formal strategic activity but an emerging process of intuitive innovative development, led by the owner-manager. The research suggests that within the size categories that are used to define small firms, it is likely that there are different types of firms with different latent propensity for growth. This work further suggests that competent owner-managers are required to develop (by using innovation heuristics they have acquired over time) and then to fulfil a multi-faceted role of entrepreneur, leader and manager, and that the degree of competence displayed has significant impact on the growth propensity of a firm.

Keywords: innovation, growth, entrepreneur, leader, manager

1 Introduction

This paper describes a piece of Systemic Action Research that was conducted with a highly specified group of owner-managed firms who had experienced significant growth after their initial formation. These types of firms are rare; as Daly et al. (1991) have pointed out less than 5% of the UK's SME population grow to employ more than twenty people after initial start up, and only approximately 15% of firms in the UK continue to trade for five years from start up (see Dunn and Bradstreet 2001). These statistics reflect the failure of the vast majority of new firms to survive after formation, and then grow to transcend the micro firm stage. They also show why the issue of growth has particular importance in this context and it also shows how innovation is constantly required to advance the development of entrepreneurial competence within such organisations.

The literature concerning the issue of growth in SME's describes a number of factors that are considered to be important. These include the type of strategic practice SME's follow, the impact of strategy on competitiveness as well as the issue of entrepreneurial activity. As a practitioner in this field this author had recognised a dissonance between much of the advocated theory and observed practice, and this prompted the study which used Soft Systems ideas (see Checkland 1981, Checkland & Scholes 1990) to consider different types of SME's, and strategic approaches the literature considered they used, as well as the significant issues that were considered to impact on the issues of competitiveness and growth.

The aim of the work was to holistically consider the issues that emerged, and then to develop a model that could be debated with a focus group of the firms involved, to get their views on the conclusions reached about how they had attained their present position. This work sought to take an original perspective and used systems ideas to shed light on the interrelationships of the identified activities and conditions. The initial findings were tested using a focus group which Curran and Blackburn (2001) have shown is a rare approach due to the difficulty of being able to recruit SME's to engage and attend these types of events.

2   Growth in SMEs

Gibb (1998) points out that the identification of a growth firm is a difficult concept to define, whilst Smallbone and North (1997) suggest that the age profile of growth firms is very difficult to establish, and that even very mature SME's have more potential for growth than is often recognised. From a policy perspective, they suggest that it may be misleading to categorise established firms as either growth firms or "trundlers," as Storey (1994) describes SME's which do not exhibit growth orientation. Clark, Berkeley and Steuer's (2003) suggest that only a minority of organisations seek to deliberately follow a growth strategy and this lack of growth focus may be exemplified by a strong commitment to independence, resulting in a stubborn "I do it my own way" individualism identified by Gibb (1998). This inordinate commitment to autonomy helps explain the common findings of a lack of strong growth ambition among many small business owners (see Curran 1986, Storey 1994, Scase & Goffee 1995). However, it does not suggest that these firms are always lacking in terms of competitiveness, or fail to utilise discernible strategic characteristics. Indeed, in order to survive they will have to maintain a degree of competitiveness; but as

Jennings and Beaver (1997) suggest, the relentless drive for personal achievement may inhibit growth potential and could ultimately impair competitiveness and therefore threaten the very survival of the firm. These views suggest that whilst most theory treats the SME community as a homogenous entity, it is in fact vastly heterogeneous in reality.

The firms researched in this work were all still managed by the founder, they had all been in existence for more than five years, and they had grown beyond the twenty person benchmark mentioned by Daly. By exceeding these two benchmarks these companies could be at least considered to be post-hoc growth firms.

3   The relationship between growth and strategy

There are numerous models (see Greiner 1972, Churchill & Lewis 1983, Scott & Bryce 1987 and Bamberger 1989) that seek to show the process of growth, most of which are based on a stage approach to growth in SME's. One of the problems with "stage of development models" is that they tend to suggest that there is continual and maintained growth and as Smallbone et al. (1993) have shown, this is not borne out by research. The implicit underlying assumption of many of these stage models would seem to be that firms face challenges concerned with maintaining competitiveness, and these are addressed through applying formal strategic management activity. Atkins and Lowe (1994) comment on the nature of strategic planning in small firms, and conclude that it may well be different from large firms, and Gibb and Scott (1985) closely link strategic planning in small firms with the management of change when considering the application of strategic activity in SME's. Carland et al. (1990) have also suggested that the planning aspect of strategic management can have a positive impact on competitiveness in SME's. These views would suggest that growth is considered to be an output of achieving a degree of competitiveness by the application of what could be considered strategic activity, orchestrated through the process of deliberate strategic management.

Stanworth and Curran (1976) took an entirely different view on growth that rejected these mostly deterministic models. They maintained that the small firm could be seen as a constructed social reality and that the owner-managers influence on strategic activity is decisive; they identified three types of potential owner-managers: the "artisan," the "classic entrepreneur," and the "manager." The authors maintained that each of these "latent social identities" has a different propensity for growth due to different levels of entrepreneurial motivation. From this perspective, strategic management and growth propensity cannot be separated from the personality-set, experience and cognitive appreciation of the owner-manager. This qualitative approach to strategic management and growth rejects neo-classical economic assumptions about the behaviour of individual firms and market economies. It does not, for example, assume that owner-managers are profit maximisers, growth-orientated, or highly competitive. Curran and Blackburn (1994) and Storey (1994) have shown all three assumptions are highly questionable for most small firms. Few owner-managers are profit maximisers, few have strong commitment to growth, and most firms operate in markets where imperfections reduce competitiveness substantially. This type of view suggests that the idea that owner-managers formally utilise strategic activity to attempt to achieve competitiveness and growth is highly questionable. Strategic management in individual firms is seen as reflecting the cognition of the owner manager reflecting Stubbs (1989) view of the importance of individual on the practice of strategic management. Embedded within this process is the practice of constant innovation that arises from the Owner Managers perception of opportunities and threats.

4 Competitiveness and SMEs

Atherton and Hannon (1996) suggest that whilst the idea of business success and growth is tangible for the small firm owner, the concept of competitiveness is abstract and vague. Gibb and Scott (1985) point out that whilst there are long lists of factors relating to competitiveness, there is an absence of theory underlying all the models that seek to integrate these factors in a useful way for SME development and education. The issue of competitiveness in SME's is not purely concerned with product and markets, but also appreciation and perception. Jennings and Beaver (1997) have pointed out that in owner-managed firms strategic management is conducted in a highly personalised way, influenced by the personality and other attributes of the owner-manager. Any strategic activity, therefore, is displayed through the leadership shown by the owner-manager, in conjunction with his/her internalised knowledge, abilities and competencies. The importance of leadership, shown in this context by the owner-manager, in relation to competitiveness and strategic management is an issue that is well recognised (see Burns 1978, Bennis & Nanus 1985, Clark & Pratt 1985). The development of leadership heuristics reflects the cognition of the owner manager and are in fact a product of cumulative innovation as the organisation develops.

Competitiveness in the small owner-managed firm sector is considered to be limited by the resources available and the willingness of the owner-manager to commit such resources to achieve a given objective. This means that the degree of competitiveness achieved can perhaps be considered to be correlated with the degree of risk owner-managers are prepared to take with the resources they have acquired, and the innovation heuristics they employ to utilise them.

5 Entrepreneurial activity and growth

There have been numerous classifications of small firm owners put forward (see Stanworth & Curran 1976, Scase & Goffee 1987, Carland et al. 1984, 1990, Jennings & Beaver 1997, and Beaver & Lashley 1998); these classifications have all followed the same basic approach of identifying owner-managers according to their propensity for entrepreneurial activity and attitude to growth. Beaver (2002) classifies these studies by suggesting three categories: "craft owners" concerned with personal satisfaction, "promoters" who want to achieve personal wealth, and "professional managers" who want to excel in business and achieve financial wealth, personal satisfaction and perhaps social status, through developing a successful business. Jennings and Beaver (1997) discuss the differences between the often quoted basic categorisation of entrepreneurs and owner-managers and suggest that as the firm grows there comes a point at which the owner-manager must delegate management responsibility to others in the organisation if the organisation is to survive and prosper. As Gerber (1995) has pointed out, this raises the issue of the three roles that the owner-manager must consider: the entrepreneur, the owner and the manager. Jennings and Beaver (1997) also suggest that as the owner-manager is the prime stakeholder, it is his/her definition of success or failure which defines the view of the firm. Success could fall substantially below the optimum level attainable (see Beaver 1984, and Foley & Green 1989); therefore perceived success is not synonymous with optimum performance. Each individual firm develops individual heuristics to operationalise the three key roles identified. The impact of innovation activity in each of these key roles is crucial to determine the level of competence the owner manager attains in each of the three areas.

Thompson (2001) suggested that strategies are a means to an end, and therefore it could be assumed that the strategies pursued by owner-managers reflect the difference between the motivations of what much of the literature considers to be owner-managers and entrepreneurs, especially in relation to growth potential.

The literature suggests that there is a wide variation in terms of the types of SME's and their approach to strategic management and strategic issues, and further suggests that there are two predominant perspectives on strategy and subsequent approaches to Strategic Management (see Eden & Ackerman 1998). The first, the prescriptive schools of thought, are based on classical economic theory reflecting observable cause and effect and the ability to be able to plan to reach desired objectives. The second, the descriptive schools, concentrate heavily on the concepts of learning, reflection and competence building which this author describes as a learning / appreciative view.

SME's can be categorised not only in terms of size but by their attitude towards growth. There is the opportunity for the classification of owner-managers into two basic groups which exhibit different attitudes to growth; "lifestyle firms" and "entrepreneurial firms." In addition leadership is identified as a key factor relating to both the issue of strategy and competitiveness, and the literature would seem to take the view that the leader of the business determines strategy which impacts on the competitiveness of the firm and the subsequent growth that is achieved.

In order to attempt to consider these views from an holistic perspective, systems ideas were employed to conceptually model the assertions regarding the types of approaches to strategy identified, as well as the process followed by "life style" or "entrepreneurial firms" in relation to growth, and the impact of leadership in this context.

6 Methodology used

6.1 Development of soft systemic paradigm

In order to investigate the perspectives identified above, Soft Systems Methodology (SSM) modelling was used. This type of approach seeks to address what the system is trying to do, how the transformation is used to achieve this, and the underlying purpose, the "why" of the system. Crucial to this type of modelling is the concept of Weltanschauung ("W") or worldview, which implicitly rejects the concept of unity of purpose. Checkland (1981) suggests that in systems thinking there are two related pairs of ideas: emergence and hierarchy, and communication and control. Wilson (1984) uses the concept of water having wetness, which has no meaning when related to hydrogen/oxygen which are its constituent parts, to explain the concept of emergence. An emergent property only has meaning at a specific level of hierarchy, and only arises when the system is working in an integrated manner above and beyond the parts that comprise it. This idea of hierarchy and systemic reduction seeks not only to isolate parts as independent wholes but to place them within the context of an interacting and emergent interdependent hierarchy. The underlying feature of the systems paradigm is the concept of "holism". Understanding of the emergent whole, through synthesis of the parts, is more meaningful in systems thinking than trying to use analysis through reductionism.

The soft perspective takes the process of systemic inquiry as being a learning system that can be used to explore the observer's perceived world. This shift of systemicity from taking the world to be systemic, to taking the process of inquiry to be systemic, is of crucial importance to the understanding of the soft systems paradigm. The hard determinative perspective that uses systematic approaches to modelling may well contain a systemic perspective of the world; however, the deterministic view of unitary purpose, and of achieving this purpose from a machine-like approach fails to account for the systemic process of inquiry that soft systems usage seeks to encompass. *In essence, "soft systems thinking" is epistemological and "hard systems thinking" is ontological.*

6.2 Applying system ideas to the area of research

Using the doubly systemic perspective of the soft systemic paradigm when considering a firm as a "human activity system" takes the process to be not only systemic, in that it can be modelled, but also doubly systemic in that such modelling can lead to learning that can be used to improve understanding of the area of review. The work undertaken used this concept to consider the area of research and to model the predominant "Ws" that emerged from the literature.

A firm is taken to be a "human activity system" that Checkland (1981) describes human activity systems as human beings taking purposeful activity.

Purposeful activity is taken to be teleological and as Stacey et al. (2000) have described there are a variety of classes of teleological action. A teleological cause is an answer to the "why" question; why does a particular phenomenon do what it does or become what it becomes? This can mean two things: the kind of movement into the future that is being assumed, and the reason for this movement in order to achieve "what." In other words, what is the purpose of the action being taken, and is it being made towards a definite goal or for a general purpose?

The description of systems and systems thinking has shown that the concept of "W" has a significant impact on how people undertake teleological activity; a process that is strongly influenced by innovation.

Ten owner managed firms who met the criteria identified earlier in this paper were selected for this study. These owner managed firms were contacted by the researcher who had extensive knowledge of the business community of Merseyside, a country in England. None of these owner managers had previously been involved in a major intervention with the researcher and the researcher personally visited each owner manager to discuss the intended project and outline the potential benefits to both the individual organisations as well as the SME sector as a whole. It is interesting that whilst an initial sample of fifty was drawn up as potential participants in this study the first ten organisations that were contacted all agreed to participate in the study after the initial visits. This in itself is an interested phenomenon as the insularity of many SME's is often quoted as a barrier to research in these types of firms (see Gibb 1998).

It was considered that whilst this work took place in a specific geographical location of Merseyside in England the fact that these owner managed firms covered a variety of business sectors including both manufacturing and service organisations and this could lead to valid observations that had application to owner managed SME's at the same stage of development throughout the UK as the Merseyside economy broadly reflects the SME distribution within the UK. It was also considered that ten firms would be a suitable sample size in which to conduct this work as it was a small enough sample to allow in depth work to be done whilst being big enough to give validity to the findings.

A structured questionnaire that had been derived from a holistic interrogation of the literature concerning growth, competitiveness and strategy was used in one to one semi-structured interviews between the researcher and the individual owner managers.

The findings from the questionnaires were grouped into emerging themes and these emerging themes were explored with the owner managers collectively in a focus group that all ten owners managers attended. The fact that these owner managers attended shows the importance they placed on the work that had been conducted, as getting owner managers to attend focus groups is notoriously difficult, as observed by Curran and Blackburn (2001).

7 Findings

During the focus group the owner-managers agreed that the growth they had attained to date was influenced by the degree of entrepreneurial activity, the willingness to take risk, and the degree of entrepreneurial empowerment that had occurred within their firms. They also agreed that they had all developed down individual pathways that bore little resemblance to each other reflecting that innovation is a process that they applied unknowingly to develop the individual heuristics that had allowed them to grow. However they also agreed that they had faced common challenges.

The findings of the focus group showed that the issue of the level of entrepreneurial activity could be considered to be not solely concerned with an individual's or firm's inherent character, as this empirical research suggests that this level of activity is never anything other than a transient state affected by the issue of the owner-managers' prevailing "W," and the level of their multi-faceted competence at different times and under different circumstances.

For example, owner-managers could iteratively move through the conceptual process shown in the figure overleaf:

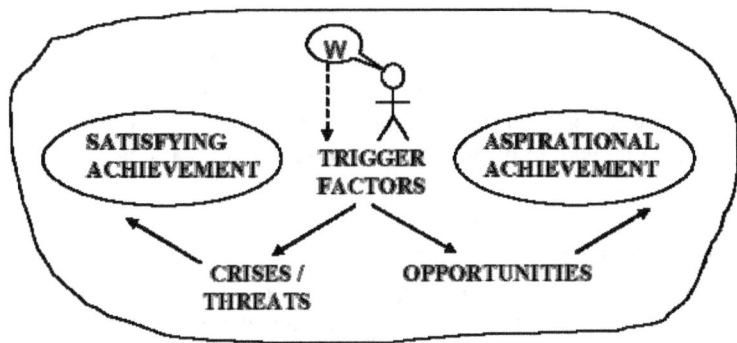

Figure 1: Iterative process of entrepreneurial action

This Figure suggests that in the light of perceived threats or opportunities, measures of performance are altered, depending on the level of potential threat or opportunity perceived. The empirical data that emerged during this research implied that growth, consolidation and survival are closely related, and are concerned with the perceived reality of the owner-managers, their "W," when considering issues within the environment that can act as "triggers" to take action. *Growth from this perspective can be taken to be a transient phenomenon reflecting the cognition and subsequent development, through innovative processes, of individual balancing heuristics in a firm.* It suggests that different trigger factors, which could be opportunities or threats perceived in the environment, can impact on the owner-managers "W" in terms of acceptable levels of performance. When facing a perceived crisis or threat, owner-managers may decide to set satisfying levels of achievement to try to ensure continuity. By contrast, if opportunities are perceived, the measures of performance may be moved to a more aspirational level, thereby stretching the organisation. Thus whilst certain individuals may be considered to inherently exhibit entrepreneurial characteristics, it is the "W" of the individual at any given time (a perception that is seen to change) that sees these changes in the perceived environment as opportunities or threats, and decides what are suitable measures of performance in the light of such perception. The "trigger factor" identification could be seen as an intuitive strategic action confirming the empirical evidence which suggests that these types of firms learn to take action at appropriate times both to maintain continuity as an ongoing activity when threats appear by limiting risk, and to use innovation to pursue growth opportunities that seem suitable to the owner-manager at a particular time.

This process is manifested within the firm through the concept of an owner-managers "vision" and its articulation. There was no evidence noted of any formal type of strategic activity within these firms and their growth can be taken to be an emergent property of the process of learning and experience over time.

8 Discussion

In terms of considering the ongoing development of a "vision," from a systems perspective, Lewis (1991) discusses the concept of appreciative systems and suggests we need to consider the importance of the internally-generated mental models of the organisation, the objectives which management use in decision-making. Rational models of decision-making, as in Simons' work (1969, 1976) critically recognised the effect of these mental models or constructs, but failed to address their nature; these mental constructs or models were recognised and addressed in the work of Vickers (1965, 1968, and 1970).

Lewis maintains that these mental models, and the process of how they change and develop, are explained through the concepts of appreciation, appreciative systems and settings formalised by Checkland and Casar (1986) shown in figure 2 overleaf:

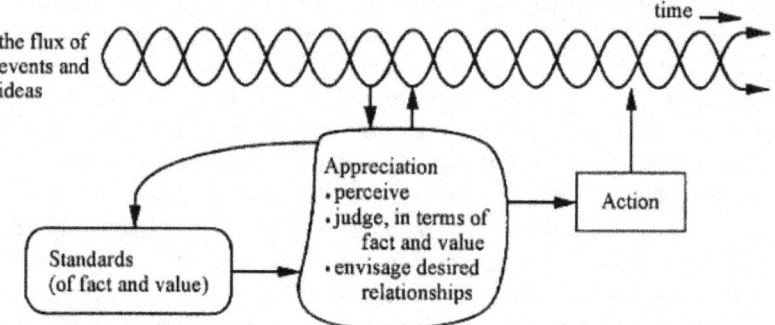

Source: After Checkland and Casar (1986)

Figure 2: Structure of appreciative system emphasising appreciative settings

At any moment in time, an appreciative system has a specific appreciative setting, which is a readiness to see and value things in one way rather than in another. *This author suggests that this statement fundamentally articu-*

lates the concept of a *"vision"* in this context, and explains how this vision is operationalised through individual heuristic developments which are the product of continuing innovation within these organisations. One of the sub-processes involved in appreciative systems is concerned with collecting data from the world and making *reality judgements* about the present situation from these. These judgements are based on what Vickers terms "norms," a term used to describe the ideas that allow organisations or individuals to understand facts and give meaning to raw data. This term could also be considered to describe a type of cultural heuristic that an organisation develops as a "lens" or "dominant logic" through which to interpret data. These norms become revealed during the operation of the appreciative system. They guide what the organisation sees and what it considers relevant. This could be taken to be a reference to tacit knowledge, potentially displayed through externalised strategic heuristics. There was little evidence of this externalisation having taken place in this research. However, the strong emphasis that the owner-managers placed on their setting of norms and values to guide their firms' actions was recognised.

This work concludes that growth is not the product of an inherent disposition, a character trait; it is the product of specific perception and reactions to on-going situations and the development of individual innovative heuristics to deal with these. "Entrepreneurs" may be more disposed to grow a firm but "lifestyle firms" can still grow if the "right" perceived circumstances are identified. This work maintains that the growth propensity of an owner-managed firm is contingent on the owner-managers appreciative settings and cognitive framework at any given point in time. Growth in this context can therefore be taken to be an emergent property of the developing of learning and enhancing of appreciation, and the subsequent action and heuristic development that is taken as time unfolds. In essence this work shows that the SME community is heterogeneous and the development of an individual firm's heuristics reflects the developing and changing cognition of the owner manager, this cognition determines their approach to innovation and its application in their own individual settings.

References
Atherton, A., & P. Hannon. (1996) "Competitiveness and Success: How the Owner-Managers of Small Firms Perceive Success in a Turbulent External Environment." 19th ISBA National Small Firms Policy and Research Conference, Birmingham, September.

Atkins, M., & J. Lowe. (1994) *International Small Business Journal*, Vol. 12, No. 3: pp. 12-24.

Bamberger, I. (1980) "Development and Growth of Firms – A Theoretical Frame of Reference For Small and Medium Firms." Unpublished Paper, University of Rennes, Department of Management.
Bamberger, I. (1989) "Developing competitive advantage in small & medium sized firms," *Long Range Planning*, Vol. 22, No. 5: pp. 80-88.
Beaver, G. (1984) "The entrepreneurial ceiling: A discussion of the small business management process," *7th UKEMRA National Small Firms Policy and Research Conference*, Nottingham, 17th September.
Beaver, G. (2002) *"Small Business, Entrepreneurship and Enterprise Development"* Pearson Education Limited: London.
Beaver, G., & C. Lashley. (1998) "Competitive advantage and management development in small hospitality firms: The need for an imaginative approach." *Journal of Vacation Marketing* Vol. 2, No 2: pp 145-60.
Bennis, W., & B. Nanus. (1985) *Leaders: The Strategies For Taking Charge*, Harper & Row: New York.
Burns, J.M. (1978) *Leadership*, Harper & Row: New York.
Carland, J.W., F. Hoy, W.R. Boulton, & J.C. Carland. (1984) "Differentiating entrepreneurs from small business owners: A conceptualisation," *Academy of Management*, Vol. 9, No. 2, pp. 354-359.
Carland, J.W., J.A.C. Carland, & C.D. Abey Jr. (1990) *International Small Business Journal*, Vol. 7, No. 4: pp. 23-44.
Checkland, P. B. (1981) *Systems Thinking, Systems practice*, J. Wiley & Sons: Chichester.
Checkland, P. B., & A. Casar. (1986) Vickers concept of an appreciative system: A systemic account. *Journal of Applied Systems Analysis*, Vol. 13, No. 3, pp: 3-17.
Checkland, P. B., & J. Scholes. (1990) *Soft systems methodology in action*, Wiley: Chichester.
Churchill, N.L., & V.L. Lewis. (1983) "The five stages of small business growth," *Harvard Business Review*, Vol. 61, No. 10: pp. 30-50
Clarke, C., & S. Pratt. (1985) "Leadership's four-part progress," *Management Today*, March 1985.
Clark, D., N. Berkeley, & N. Steuer. (2003) 'Attitudes to growth among owners of small and medium-sized enterprises and the implications for business advice', *International Small Business Journal*, Vol. 19, No. 3
Curran, J. (1986) *"Bolton 15 years, on: A review and analysis of small business research in Britain 1971-1986,"* Small Business Research Trust: London.
Curran, J., & R.A. Blackburn. (1994) *"Small firms and local economic networks, the death of the local economy,"* Paul Chapman: London.
Curran, J., & A. Blackburn. (2001) *Researching the Small Enterprise*, Sage: London
Daly, M., M. Campbell, G. Robson, & C. Gallagher. (1991) "Job creation 1987-9: The contribution of small and large firms," *Employment Gazette*, November: pp. 589-596.
Davidson, P. (1991) "Continued entrepreneurship: ability, need and opportunity as determinants of small firm growth," *Journal of Business Venturing*, Vol. 6, No. 8: pp. 405-429.
Dunn and Bradstreet. (2001) *Commercial statistics report*, London.
Eden, C., & F. Ackermann. (1998) *Strategy Making: The journey of strategic management*, Sage: London.
Foley, P., & H. Green. (1989) *Small Business Success*, Paul Chapman, London.
Gerber, M.E. (1995) The E-myth revisited. New York: HarperCollins.

Leading Issues in Innovation Research

Gibb, A. (1998) "Academic research and the growth of ignorant SME Policy: Mythical concepts, myths, assumptions, rituals and confusions," Paper presented to the National Small Firms Policy and Research Conference, Durham, 16th November

Gibb, A., & L. Davies. (1992) "Development of a growth model," *The Journal of Entrepreneurship*, Vol. 1, No. 1: pp. 3-36.

Gibb, A., & M. Scott. (1985) "Strategic awareness, personal commitment and the process of planning in the small business," *Journal of Management Studies*, Vol. 22, No. 6: pp. 597-632.

Greiner, L.E. (1972) "Evolution and revolution as organisations grow," *Harvard Business Review*, Vol. 50, No. 4: pp. 66-78.

Jennings, P., & G. Beaver. (1997) "The performance and competitive advantage of small firms: A management perspective," *International Small Business Journal*, Vol. 15, No. 2: pp. 21-34.

Lewis, P.J. (1991) "The decision making basis for information systems: the contribution of Vickers" concept of appreciation to the soft systems perspective," *European Journal of Information Systems*, Vol. 1, No. 1: pp. 33-43.

Perren, L. (1999) "Factors in the growth of micro-enterprises (part 1): Developing a framework," *Journal of Small Business and Enterprise Development*, Vol. 6, No. 4: pp. 12-19.

Scase, R., & R. Goffee. (1987) *The Real World of the Small Business Owner*, (2nd edition) Beckenham: Croom Helm.

Scase, R., & R. Goffee. (1995) *Corporate realities: The Dynamics of Large and Small Organisations*, Routledge: London

Scott, M., & R. Bryce. (1987) "Five stages of growth in small business," *Long Range Planning*, Vol. 20, No. 3: pp. 45-52.

Simon, H.A. (1969) *The sciences of the artificial*, MIT Press: Cambridge, Mass.

Simon, H.A. (1976) "From substantive to procedural rationality," in H.A. Simon, (Ed.) *Models of bounded rationality: Behavioural economics and business organisation*, MIT Press: Cambridge, Mass.

Smallbone, D.J., D. North, & R. Leigh. (1993) "The growth and survival of mature manufacturing SME's in the 1980's: an urban-rural comparison," in D. Storey and J. Curran (Eds.), *Small Firms in Urban and Rural Locations*, Routledge: London.

Smallbone, D., & D. North. (1997) Targeting established SME's: Does their age matter," *International Small Business Journal*, Vol. 13, No. 3 : pp. 16-28.

Stacey, R.D., D. Griffin, & P. Shaw. (2000) *Complexity and management: Fad or radical challenge to systems thinking?*, Routledge: London.

Stanworth, J., & J. Curran. (1976) "Growth and the small firm – An alternative view," *Journal of Management Studies*, Vol. 13, No. 2: pp. 95-110.

Storey, D.J. (1994) *Understanding the Small Business Sector*, Routledge: London.

Stubbart, C.I. (1989) "Managerial Cognition: A Missing Link in Strategic Management Research". *Journal of Management Studies*.

Thompson, J.L. (2001) *Strategic management* (4th edition), Thomson Learning: London.

Thompson, J. (2006) *Enabling Entrepreneurs*, University of Huddersfield.

Vickers, G. (1965) *The art of judgement*, Chapman and Hall: London.

Vickers, G. (1968) *Value systems and social process*, Tavistock; London.

Vickers, G. (1970) *Freedom in a rocking boat*, Allen Lane: London.

Wilson, B. (1984) *Systems: Concepts, methodologies and applications*, Wiley: Chichester.

Paul Donaldson

Inter-Firm Alliances: A Mechanism to Develop Innovative Capacity in Portuguese SMEs

Luís Valentim[1], Mário Franco[2] and João Lisboa[1]
[1]Management Department, School of Economics, University of Coimbra, Coimbra, Portugal
[2]NECE-Research Center in Business Sciences, Management and Economics Department, University of Beira Interior, Covilhã, Portugal
Originally published in The Proceedings of ECIE 2012

Editorial commentary

In this paper, Valentim, Franco and Lisboa discuss a study of inter-firm alliances among SMEs drawn from a range of sectors in the Portuguese business community, including the service sector. They focus particularly on the motives for the formation of such alliances, and set out to determine the extent to which a desire or need to innovate acts as a driver for SMEs to enter inter-firm alliances.

Some points for discussion, learning and reflection arising from this paper include:
- The potential benefits of forming alliances with other SMEs.
- The potential dangers or pitfalls of forming alliances with other SMEs.
- Alternatives to forming alliances in order to innovate and grow.
- response to challenges
- The organisational and managerial skills required to forge effective inter-firm alliances.

Abstract: Nowadays, innovation plays a key role in a company's survival in an innovation-driven economy. Inter-firm alliances allow Small and Medium Enterprises (SMEs) to develop critical capabilities for growth and innovation through access to external resources and knowledge which are otherwise unavailable. At present, inter-firm alliances are an innovation-generating procedure, challenging SMEs' learning and entrepreneurship skills in order to create new products and services. The main research objectives of this paper are: (i) to identify and categorize factors that SMEs take into account when deciding to enter an inter-firm alliance; (ii) verify the importance of innovation-related motives; and (iii) measure the influence of firms' characteristics on SMEs' motives. A total of 4.534 SMEs supplied by the Informa D&B Portugal database was surveyed by email. Data was collected in June and September 2011 through an online questionnaire. A total of 260 completed questionnaires were returned, yielding a response rate of 5.73%. For measurement, we used the Haase and Franco (2011) scale of importance with addition of the "knowledge acquisition and transfer" variable (Kogut, 1988). The principal business activities of SMEs in the sample are services (52.3%), manufacturing (43.8%) and agriculture (3.8%), and 62.6% of respondents were involved in alliances with other firms. The motives for entering inter-firm alliances were defined through exploratory factor analysis using the method of principal components and the varimax rotation method with Kaiser normalisation. The analysis grouped the variables into three different factors, explaining 67.2% of the total variance. Factor 1: "Innovation, learning and knowledge acquisition and transfer"; Factor 2: "Operational improvements and reaching competitive advantage"; Factor 3: "Entering new markets and improving and maintaining market share". The KMO found was 0.878 and the smallest Cronbach's alpha 0.842, which guarantees high reliability of the psychometric instruments. Using the one-way ANOVA several significant differences were found between manufacturing and service industries as well as between firms focusing on the domestic and export markets. Also innovation, efficiency and competitiveness appear to be the main factors driving SMEs' cooperation.

Keywords: motives, inter-firm alliances, innovation, SMEs, Portugal

1 Introduction

Small and Medium Enterprises (SMEs), due to their lack of resources (Okamuro, 2007) and liabilities of smallness (Aldrich and Auster, 1986), newness (Baum and Oliver, 1991) and connectedness (Rickne, 2006), have more difficulty dealing with fast technological change and product innovation than big companies.

In this context, for Teng (2007), inter-firm alliances play a key role in growth and entrepreneurial development activities, namely in innovation, new firm creation and corporate renewal. In fact, firm skills and external cooperation are not substitutes, but complement each other. Inter-firm alliances allow SMEs to develop critical capabilities for growth and innovation through access to external resources and knowledge which are otherwise unavailable (Khana, Gulati and Nohria, 1998). At present, inter-firm alliances are an innovation-generating procedure, challenging SMEs' learning and entrepreneurship skills in order to create new products and services (Liou and Liou, 2009).

According to Harrison et al (2001), firms should look for complementary resources in order to make up for internal weaknesses. However, after doing this they should exploit synergies between their original skills and those of their partners. For Welbourne and Pardo-del-Val (2009), the most successful firms will be those able to build relational capital to face the increasing speed of change. To be competitive and exploit new opportunities, entrepreneurs need resources they do not have most of the time. This builds pressure on them to build formal and informal relations with firms and entrepreneurs, that is, they are forced to negotiate and cooperate.

Santamaria, Nieto and Gil (2009) concluded that technological innovation benefits the activities of SMEs in low and medium technological sectors and Barge-Gil (2010) points out that SMEs and firms outside the high-tech sectors are those benefiting most from cooperation to foster their innovation activities. Nieto and Santamaria (2010) confirmed that technological collaboration is a critical factor for SMEs to improve innovativeness, especially product oriented innovation.

Gnyawali and Park (2009) argue that the study of innovation and cooperative alliances with competitors has been focused on big companies. The conclusions of Barge-Gil (2010) refute the idea that firms with strong networks, meaning large firms and firms with a technological profile, the focus of previous studies, give more value to inter-firm alliances. In fact, SMEs are the ones establishing inter-firm alliances to develop new products and processes. Thus, for the purpose of this study, we define inter-firm alliances (formalized or not) as a mutual and voluntary decision adopted by two or more independent firms in order to trade or share resources for mutual benefit.

In spite of the opportunities that might go along with inter-firm alliances, there is only limited empirical evidence of the impact of this strategy on SMEs. Against this background, we believe that more systematic empirical research is necessary as there are many unanswered questions regarding the motives for these types of entrepreneurial relationships. This applies in particular to SMEs. Therefore, the main research objectives of this paper are: (i) to identify and categorize factors that SMEs take into account when deciding to enter an inter-firm alliance; (ii) verify the importance of innovation-related motives; and (iii) measure the influence of firms' characteristics on SMEs' motives.

This study makes several contributions to the study of inter-firm alliances: (i) it is an empirical investigation of Portuguese SMEs' motives for entering inter-firm alliances; (ii) it targets various sectors, including services and agriculture, which is quite rare and may bring new insights to the field of SME inter-firm alliance studies; (iii) it identifies and categorizes factors regarding how Portuguese SMEs evaluate motives for alliance formation; (iv) it measures the influence of firms' characteristics on SMEs' motives for alliance formation.

2 Theoretical background

Our study seeks to extend the findings of previous inter-firm alliance literature and more particularly the motives for SMEs entering into such agreements.

2.1 Inter-firm alliances

For Gulati (1998), inter-firm alliances are voluntary agreements between firms that exchange or share resources and engage together in the development of products, services or technologies. There are two types of alliances: pooling and complementary, the latter characterised by decreasing levels of resource similarity (Das and Teng, 2000). According to Smith, Carrol and Ashford (1995), alliances can be formal, characterised by contractual duties and formal structures of control, and informal, flexible agreements controlled by behavioural norms. Besides, they can be vertical, with suppliers or customers, and horizontal, when involving competitors. For Culpan (2009), alliances can be bilateral when engaging two firms, or multiple relations when engaging three firms or more.

According to Todeva and Knoke (2005), alliances are organizational forms between markets and hierarchies that combine different degrees of market interaction and bureaucratic integration.

For Menard (2006), alliances are market substitutes because markets are unable to promote the right combination of resources and skills. Also, firm integration (hierarchy) would reduce flexibility and weaken incentive regimes. He concludes that combining resources only makes sense based on the assumption of a continuous relationship between alliance members.

Eisenhardt and Scoonhoven (1996) argue also that alliances are cooperative relations that follow a logic of strategic resource needs and opportunities of social resources. Inter-firm alliance formation for entrepreneurial firms lies in a combination of a vulnerable strategic position (new markets, technological innovation) and the strong social position of management teams (strong environmental ties and social status).

Building strong ties with large companies is vital for SMEs' growth, because due to their lack of resources SMEs need large companies to finance new product development and to implement marketing strategies to overcome the liability of smallness (Stuart, 2000).

Morris, Koçak and Ozer (2007) also concluded that cooperation among SMEs is very common, even within the same business. Trust and commitment are the key factors for success, as happens with non-competitors. Mutual benefits are critical in this type of agreement, namely benefits related to resources, information and market position.

For Khana, Gulati and Nohria (1998) alliances allow private and social benefits. The first are those earned unilaterally by the company learning from partners' skills and applying them in areas unrelated to the alliance. The second are those each partner receives from collective application of both partners' knowledge in areas related to the alliance. When the ratio of private to common benefits is low, the alliance is closer to a pure cooperation model.

Papadopoulos, Cimon and Hébert (2008) studied how heterogeneity and asymmetry impact on firms' relations. Too much heterogeneity may imply a loss of synergies, while too much asymmetry may lead to opportunistic behaviour. Parkhe (1993) argues that opportunistic behaviour may inhibit cooperation. Cooperation can only be strong when firms take into account longer time horizons, interact more frequently and behave more transparently.

The impact and share of gains resulting from asymmetric partners is a key issue for SMEs. Indeed, SMEs are generally the weakest link in an alliance made with large companies. However, studies have concluded there are always gains for both parties in different alliance focuses, namely in R&D, new product development, marketing and licensing agreements. Accordingly, partner asymmetry is not an obstacle per se to alliance formation due to concerns of appropriation by alliance partners (McConnell and Nantell, 1985; Das, Sen and Sengupta, 1998; Alvarez and Barney, 2001).

2.2 Motives for entering inter-firm alliances

Pfeffer and Novak (1976) argue that firms enter into alliances to deal with two kinds of interdependencies; competitive and symbiotic. For Contractor and Lorange (1988), alliances have different goals: risk reduction, achieving economies of scale, technology transfer, blocking competitors and facilitating international expansion. According to Kogut (1988), alliances are made to deal with small scale bargaining situations, strengthen competitive advantage and transfer and acquire organizational knowledge.

Hagedoorn (1993) studied the motives for forming inter-firm alliances in the area of technology and found a correlation between the growing complexity of technological developments and the use of external sources through formation of technological alliances. So external resources for renewal and innovation complement firms' endogenous skills and allow them to deal with complex technologies through resource sharing, generating learning and innovation capabilities, reducing the time to market and easing access to external markets.

Dyer and Singh (1998) concluded that alliance formation has the following advantages: knowledge exchange, combination of scarce and complementary resources to generate new products, services or technologies, and lower transaction costs due to more efficient governance mechanisms. However, for Gulati (1999), the focus on resources and capabilities as motives for alliance formation underestimated the role of social motives which may play a decisive role.

2.3 Inter-firm alliances and innovation in SMEs

According to Shan, Walker and Kogut (1994) there are opportunities for cooperation between SMEs and large firms in emerging industries for exploiting technological knowledge and resource transfer for product commercialization. They concluded that SMEs' output and their cooperation agreements are not mutually reciprocal and innovation is explained by inter-firm alliances.

Belderbos, Carree and Loshkin (2006) studied cooperative R&D and concluded that its results change as a function of the partner and that knowledge exchanges are strong incentives to form inter-firm alliances. Alliances with customers result in tailor-made products and alliances with suppliers are more focused on cost reduction.

As stated by Pittaway *et al.* (2004), the benefits associated with innovation through participation in inter-firm alliances are: (i) risk sharing, (ii) access to new markets and technologies, (iii) quicker access to the market when launching new products, (iv) combination of complementary resources and protection of property rights when it is not possible to sign complete contracts.

Franco (2003) studied cooperation among SMEs as a mechanism to innovate. Innovation and organizational learning are the first motive for entering inter-firm alliances among Portuguese SMEs. For Okamuro (2007), cooperation in R&D allows SMEs` access to external resources, to achieve synergies and economies of scale, and reduce risk and waste resulting from duplication of efforts.

Gnyawali and Park (2009) studied the correlation between technological innovation in SMEs and predisposition to cooperate with competitors. They found that resource utility is an important factor in forming inter-firm alliances due to similarity of use and target markets.. At the same time competitors face the same type of external pressures, namely technological change and the need for strong investment in R&D.

3 Research methodology

3.1 Sample
The target population was Portuguese SMEs, based on a list of firms generated by *Informa D&B* Portugal. SMEs were defined according to the European Union (EU) definition based on number of employees and sales turnover. Micro companies (fewer than 10 employees) were not considered in the study. The principal business activities of SMEs in the sample are services (52.3%), manufacturing (43.8%) and agriculture (3.8%). 62.6%

of respondents were involved in alliances with other firms. Furthermore, 71.5% of the firms have between 10 and 49 employees, 63.5% are more than 20 years old and exports represent less than 5% of sales in 63.1% of firms, as a consequence of their focus on the domestic market. The most frequent types of inter-firm alliances are marketing and distribution agreements, and outsourcing and informal agreements. Partners are primarily suppliers, followed by customers and competitors. The main functional areas of agreement are commercial and marketing, followed by technical and production. R&D, quality and logistics are not so important.

3.2 Data collection

A total of 4534 firms were contacted by email. Data collection was made in June and September 2011 through an online questionnaire. This questionnaire was sent to the owner-manager or administrator of the previously selected firms. A pre-test was carried out in the presence of the respondents. After making the changes resulting from this process, a new pre-test was carried out online replicating the conditions of the questionnaire. The respondents of the pre-tests were excluded. A total of 260 usable completed questionnaires were returned, yielding a response rate of 5.73%. The low response rate can be explained by the following reasons: (i) small firms may find it more difficult to reply to email questionnaires than bigger companies (ii) small firms' managers have a limited amount of time to devote to these matters as well as limited human resources. For measurement, we used the Haase and Franco (2011) scale of importance with addition of the "knowledge acquisition and transfer" variable (Kogut, 1988). In this case we used a seven-point Likert scale ranging from Not at all important (1) to Extremely important (7).

3.3 Data analysis

To reach the research goals we used different statistical analyses. We carried out a statistical descriptive analysis followed by exploratory factor analysis. Based on the latter method, we were able to reduce the number of variables and combine them in factors which can explain why SMEs enter inter-firm alliances. In order to check the acceptability of the technique, we used the Kaiser-Meyer-Olkin (KMO) measure of sampling adequacy and the Bartlett Test of Sphericity. The internal consistency of the scale and the level of consistency between variables were measured by the Cronbach's alpha reliability analysis. In order to check the influence of firm characteristics on the three factors explaining the motives for entering inter-firm alliances, we used a one-way ANOVA test.

4 Results and discussion

4.1 Clustering of alliance formation factors

The mean values of the different motives for inter-firm alliances have higher values than the mean of the scale, which is logical due to the fact that the respondents are companies that entered into some type of inter-firm alliance (Table 1).

Table 1: Alliance formation motives (factor analysis)

Variables	Mean	Factor Loadings
Factor 1: Innovation, learning and knowledge acquisition and transfer		
To improve innovation	5.31	0.846
To improve quality	5.54	0.836
Technology transfer	4.63	0.724
To foster the learning process	5.04	0.759
To share resources and competencies	5.50	0.615
Knowledge acquisition and transfer	5.21	0.673
Factor 2: Operational improvements and reaching competitive advantage		
To create economies of scale	5.23	0.688
To reduce transaction costs	5.16	0.799
Risk sharing	4.64	0.634
To improve lead times	5.25	0.728
To explore and create synergies	5.35	0.711
To achieve competitive advantage	5.77	0.539
Factor 3: Entering new markets and market power		
To enter new markets	5.56	0.788
To increase market share	5.82	0.864
To consolidate market position	5.68	0.804

Note: The mean for individual criteria is the average on a scale: 1 – Not at all important; 2 – Low importance; 3 – Slightly important; 4 – Neutral; 5 – Moderately important; 6 – Very important; 7- Extremely important; Varimax rotational procedure was used. Only values above 0.5 are presented

The variables of the scale were reduced to three factors through exploratory factor analysis using principal component analysis as the extraction method and Varimax rotation with Kaiser Normalisation. Items with eigenvalues greater than 1.0 were extracted (Table 2). This table shows three factors of SME motives for alliance formation: (1) Innovation, learning and knowledge acquisition and transfer; (2) Operational improvements and competitive advantage; (3) Entering new markets and market power.

Next, we describe and explain in detail the factors mentioned above.

Table 2: Statistical values

	Factor 1	Factor 2	Factor 3
Eigenvalues	6.998	1.736	1.344
Percentage of explained variance	26.093	21.366	19.728
Percentage of cumulative variance	26.093	47.459	67.188
Cronbach´s Alpha	0.898	0.844	0.846

Notes: N=163, KMO=0.877, Bartlett´s test: 1495.072, df=105 and Sig. Level: p=0.000

Innovation, learning and knowledge acquisition and transfer

This factor appears as Portuguese SME´s main motive for entering inter-firm alliances. This confirms that SMEs are aware of their endogenous limitations, translated into resource scarcity and liabilities of size, age and connectedness. In order to cope with challenges posed by changing competitive environments, consumer preferences and continuous innovation, the strategic alternative for SMEs is to combine their resources and skills with other firms and in doing so, be better prepared to compete in global markets offering new products, services or technologies (Dyer and Sigh, 1998). These findings confirm the conclusions of Franco (2003) that innovation is the main factor explaining SME alliance formation and those of Shan, Walker and Kogut (1994), that innovation in SMEs is explained by cooperation alliances. At the same time, and due to the fact that we live in a knowledge-based economy, knowledge acquisition and transfer from external sources appears as an absolute necessity for SMEs, as predicted by Belderbos, Carree and Loshkin (2006).

Operational improvements and reaching competitive advantage

This factor translates SMEs' concerns about efficiency. It groups variables related to competitiveness factors such as cost (economies of scale, transaction costs) and time (lead times). This factor deals with the execution issues faced by SMEs. Nowadays, it is not enough to have good products. Firms must produce at competitive prices and deliver those products on time. These necessary conditions are not easy to achieve. They require investment in people and technology and building up internal capabilities and know-how. Liabilities of size put pressure on SMEs to reach these goals. They are in a disadvantageous position due to financing difficulties and their capacity to attract young talent compared to big companies that can offer more attractive careers. These findings are in line with the conclusions of (Contractor and Lorange, 1988; Dyer and Singh, 1998; Okamuro, 2007).

Entering new markets and market power

Competitive rivalry has never before reached the present levels. It is difficult to enter new markets, and equally difficult to increase or defend market positions. This involves many resources of different kinds: human, financial, marketing and technical. It puts a lot of pressure on SMEs' organizational resources and capabilities. Partnering is an obvious solution to all these challenges. Partnering may be the only solution due to the fact that standing alone, SMEs are not able to meet these challenges. Awareness of their strengths and weaknesses is a vital step for SMEs in dealing with their environment. These findings are in line with the conclusions of (Contractor and Lorange, 1988; Pittaway *et al.*, 2004).

4.2 The influence of a firm's characteristics on alliance formation motives

In order to check the influence of firm characteristics on the three factors that explain the motives for entering inter-firm alliances, and despite the lack of normality, we used a one-way ANOVA test. In fact, the absolute values of kurtosis and skewness are well below 3 for skewness and 10 for kurtosis, meaning that we are not facing serious violation of the assumption of normality (Kline, 2004). Accordingly, we used parametric tests (Tables 3 and 4). Based on the results, we used a Turnkey test for multiple comparisons.

Table 3: Sector of activity on alliance motives (Anova)

Factors	Sector of activity	N	F	p
Innovation, learning and knowledge acquisition and transfer	Manufacturing	76	3.615	0.029
	Services	81		
	Agriculture	6		

Table 4: Exports on alliance motives (Anova)

Factors	Exports	N	F	p
Innovation, learning and knowledge acquisition and transfer	Do not export	44	3.048	0.012
	Up to 5%	54		
	5% to 10%	12		
	10% to 25%	15		
	25% to 50%	8		
	More than 50%	30		

Using a one-way ANOVA test we concluded that sector of activity and exports have a statistically significant influence ($p<0.05$) on the innovation, learning and knowledge acquisition and transfer factor in forming inter-firm alliances. Based on this, we applied a Tukey test of multiple comparisons and a statistically significant difference ($p<0.05$) was found between manufacturing and services, with the services mean being greater than that of manufacturing. A Tukey test was also applied to exports and we found a statistically significant difference ($p<0.05$) between firms focused on the domestic market (exports less than 5% of total sales) and firms whose exports represent 10% to 25%. The former give more importance to the innovation, learning and knowledge acquisition and transfer factor than the latter.

These results point to the fact that in a service-driven economy SMEs are faced with greater challenges than manufacturing firms. The degree of innovation in the service sector is continuously growing leveraged by the advances in technology, mainly the internet. One possible explanation for the fact that firms focused on the domestic market are those attributing more importance to the innovation, learning, knowledge and acquisition factor, is that those firms face a shrinking domestic market, suffer the competitive rivalry of subsidiaries of large multinational companies that export their best practices around the world and consequently raise the bar on the competitive level, and therefore feel most need to innovate, learn and absorb knowledge from external sources.

5 Concluding remarks

For SMEs, establishing inter-firm alliances has become a strategic alternative to deal with a complex and changing environment. Poor in resources and skills, SMEs have to cooperate in order to be able to respond to the challenges they face in current markets. We could say to partner or to die. Alliance formation is a viable solution to be effective, efficient and competitive. The challenge faced by SMEs must be met by an organizational response from SME owners and managers. The soft skills needed to do so are very different from the hard skills they were used to in the past.

As a general conclusion, we may say that Portuguese SMEs are aware of the challenges they face. Two thirds of the SMEs studied have entered some type of alliance in order to respond to different challenges. Those challenges are well-defined: to innovate and to be efficient and competitive. The SMEs giving most importance to inter-firm alliance formation are those belonging to the service sector and those most focused on the domestic market.

This study contributes to the study of the motives for alliance formation in several ways: (i) it is an empirical study of Portuguese SMEs' alliance formation motives; (ii) it studies different sectors, principally the service sector, which has not been the focus of studies in this area; (iii) it identifies and categorizes factors regarding how Portuguese SMEs evaluate alliance formation motives; (iv) it measures the influence of firms' characteristics on SMEs' alliance formation motives.

References

Aldrich, H. and Auster, E. (1986) "Even dwarfs started small: liabilities of age and size and their strategic implications", in Staw, B.M. and Cummings, L.L. (Eds.): *Research in Organizational Behavior*, Vol. 8, pp.165–198, JAI Press, Greenwich, CT.

Alvarez, S. and Barney, J.(2002) "Resource-Based Theory and the Entrepreneurial Firm". in Hitt, M., Ireland, R., Camp, S. and Sexton, D. (Eds.): *Strategic Entrepreneurship: Creating a New Mindset*, pp. 89-105, Blackwell Publishers, Oxford.

Barge-Gil, A. (2010) "Cooperation-based innovators and peripheral cooperators: An empirical analysis of their characteristics and behavior", *Technovation*, Vol. 30, No. 3, pp. 195-206

Baum, J. and Oliver, C. (1991) "Institutional Linkages and Organizational Mortality", *Administrative Science Quarterly*, Vol. 36, No. 2, pp. 187-218.

Belderbos, R., Carree, M. and Loshkin, B. (2006) "Complementarity in R&D Cooperation Strategies", *Review of Industrial Organization*, Vol. 28, No. 4, pp. 401-426.

Contractor, F. e Lorange, P. (1988) "Why should firms cooperate?The Strategy and Economics Basis for Cooperative Ventures". in Contractor, F. and Lorange, P. (Eds.): *Cooperative*

Strategies in International Business: Joint Ventures and Technological Partnerships Between Firms, pp. 3-30, Elsevier Science, Oxford.

Culpan, R.(2009) "A fresh look at strategic alliances: research issues and future directions", *International Journal of Strategic Business Alliances*, Vol. 1, No. 1, pp. 4-23.

Das, T. and Teng, B. (2000) "A Resource-Based Theory of Strategic Alliances", *Journal of Management*, Vol. 26, No. 1, pp. 31-61.

Das, S., Sen .P. and Sengupta, S. (1998) "Impact of strategic alliances on firm valuation", *Academy of Management Journal*, Vol. 41, No. 1, pp. 27-41.

Dyer, J. and Singh, H. (1998) "The Relational View: Cooperative Strategy and Sources of Interorganizational Competitive Advantage" *Academy of Management Review*, Vol. 23, No. 4, pp. 660-679.

Eisenhardt, K and Schoonhoven, C. (1996) "Resource-Based View of Strategic Alliance Formation: Strategic and Social Effects in Entrepreneurial Firms", *Organization Science*, Vol. 7, No. 2, pp. 136-150.

Franco, M. (2003) "Collaboration among SMEs as a Mechanism for Innovation: An Empirical Study", *New England Journal of Entrepreneurship*, Vol. 6, No. 1, pp. 23-32.

Gnyawali, D. and Park, B. (2009) "Co-opetition and Technological Innovation in Small and Medium-Sized Enterprises: A Multilevel Conceptual Model", *Journal of Small Business Management*, Vol.47, No.3, pp. 308-330.

Gulati, R. (1998) "Alliances and Networks", *Strategic Management Journal*, Vol. 19, No. 4, pp. 293-317

Gulati, R. (1999) "Network Location and Learning: The Influence of Network Resources and Firm Capabilities on Alliance Formation", *Strategic Management Journal*, Vol. 20, pp. 397-420.

Haase, H. and Franco, M.(2011) "An exploratory study of the motives and perceived effectiveness of international cooperative alliances among SMEs", *International Journal of Enterpreneurship and Innovation Management*, Vol.13, No.3/4, pp. 314-336.

Hagedoorn, J. (1993) "Understanding the Rationale of Strategic Technology Partnering: Interorganizational Modes of Cooperation and Sectoral Differences", *Strategic Management Journal*, Vol. 14, No. 5, pp. 371-385.

Harrison,J., Hiit, M., Hoskisson, R. and Ireland, R. (2001) "Resouce Complementarity in Business Combinations: Extending the Logic to Organizational Alliances", *Journal of Management*, Vol. 27, No. 6, pp. 679-690.

Khanna,T., Gulati,R. and Nohria, N. (1998) "The Dynamics of Learning Alliances: Competition, Cooperation, and Relative Scope", *Strategic Management Journal*, Vol.19, No. 3, pp. 193-210.

Kogut, B. (1988) "Joint ventures: Theoretical and empirical perspectives", Strategic Management Journal, Vol. 9, No. 4, pp. 319-332

Kline, R.(2004) *"Principles and Practice of Structural Equation Modeling"*, New York: Guilford Press.

Liou, D. and Liou, J. (2009) "The structure and evolution of knowledge clusters: a system perspective", *International Journal of Technology Management*, Vol. 46, No. 3/4, pp. 307-325.

McConnell, J. and Nantell, T. (1985) "Corporate Combinations and Commons Stock Returns", *The Journal of Finance*, Vol.40, No. 2, pp. 519-536.

Menard,C. (2006) "Hybrid Organization of Production and Distribution" *Revista de Análisis Económico*, Vol. 21, No. 2, pp. 25-41.

Morris, M., Koçak, A. and Ozer, A. (2007) "Coopetition as a small business strategy: Implications for performance", *Journal of Small Business Strategy*, Vol. 18, No. 1, pp. 35-55.

Nieto, M. and Santamaria, L. (2010) "Technological Collaboration: Bridging the Innovation Gap between Small and Large Firms", *Journal of Small Business Management*, Vol. 48, No.1, pp. 44-69

Okamuro, H. (2007) "Determinants of success R&D cooperation in Japanese small businesses: The impact of organizational and contractual characteristics", *Research Policy*, Vol. 36, No. 10, pp. 1529-1544.

Papadopoulos, A., Cimon, A. and Hébert, (2008)"Asymmetry, heterogeneity, and inter-firm relationships", *International Journal of Organizational Analysis*, Vol. 16, No.1/2, pp. 152-165.

Parkhe, A. (1993) "Strategic Alliance Structuring: A Game Theoretic and Transaction Cost Examination of Interfirm Cooperation", *Academy of Management Journal*, Vol. 36, No. 4, pp. 794-829.

Pfeffer, J. and Nowak, P. (1976) „Joint Ventures and Interorganizational Interdependence" *Administrative Science Quarterly*, Vol. 21, No. 3, pp. 398-418.

Pittaway, L., Robertson, M., Munir, K., Danyer, D. and Neely, A. (2004) "Networking and Innovation: A Systematic Review of the Evidence", *International Journal of Management Reviews*, Vol.5/6, No. 3/4, pp. 137-168.

Rickne, A. (2006)"Connectivity and Performance of Science-based Firms", *Small Business Economics*, Vol. 26, No. 4, pp. 393-407.

Santamaria, L., Nieto, M. and Barge-Gil, A. (2009) "Beyond formal R&D: Taking advantage of other sources of innovation in low-and medium- technology industries", *Research Policy*, Vol. 38, No.3, pp. 507-517

Shan, W., Walker, G. and Kogut, B. (1994)"Interfirm cooperation and startup innovation in the biotechnology industry", *Strategic Management Journal*, Vol. 15, Nº 5, pp. 387-394.

Smith. K., Carroll. S. and Ashford, S. (1995) "Intra and Interorganizacional Cooperation: Toward a Research Agenda", *Academy of Management Journal*, Vol. 38, No. 1, pp. 7-23.

Stuart, T. (2000) "Interorganizational alliances and the performance of firms: a study of growth and innovation rates in a high technology industry", *Strategic Management Journal*, Vol. 21, No. 8, pp. 791-811.

Teng, B. (2007) "Corporate Entrepreneurship Activities through Strategic Alliances: A Resource-Based Approach toward Competitive Advantage", *Journal of Management Studies*, Vol. 44, No. 1, pp. 119-142.

Todeva, E. and Knoke, D.(2005) "Strategic alliances and models of collaboration", *Management Decision*, Vol. 43, No. 1, pp. 123-148.

Welbourne, T. and Pardo-del-Val, M. (2009) "Relational Capital: Strategic Advantage for Small and Medium-Size Enterprises (SMEs) Through Negotiation and Collaboration", *Group Decision and Negotiation*, Vol.18, No. 5, pp. 483-497.

Luís Valentim, Mário Franco and João Lisboa

Service Innovation: A Smaller Firm Perspective

Edward McKeever, Sarah Jack and Danny Soetanto
Lancaster University Management School
Originally published in The Proceedings of ECIE 2011

Editorial commentary
In this paper, McKeever, Jack and Soetanto present a thought-provoking discussion of service innovation, and explore how service innovations are generated and developed. They highlight the growing importance of service innovation in post-industrial economies, and provide an overview of some of the key differences between product and service innovation. Drawing on the literature of organisational learning, the authors seek to understand service innovation as an adaptive learning process, and examine the phenomenon through a "learning lens". The insights in to service innovation presented in the paper are informed from in-depth interviews with an entrepreneur in a logistics and freight forwarding business.

Some points for discussion, learning and reflection arising from this paper include:
- Service innovation as an adaptive learning process.
- The nature of the service innovation environment or context.
- The role of the entrepreneur in leading and shaping service innovation.
- The role of the entrepreneur's network in generating and developing service innovations.
- The importance of stakeholder relationships in developing effective service innovations.

Abstract: Since the term service innovation first emerged, concerns have been raised about the merging of the two concepts (i.e. service and innovation). The purpose of this paper is to contribute to this debate and broaden understanding about what the term might actually mean. To do so we consider what goes on between entrepreneurial firms and their environments so that service innovations are brought about. We argue that through environmental enactment and organisational learning, entrepreneurial firms actively 'generate' service innovations and turn ideas into purposeful changes in the way services are delivered. They do this by developing and acting upon a deep and interactive understanding of their customers as well as their wider environments. We therefore propose that service innovation is best understood as a highly social process whereby firms seek to improve their performance based on interactive knowledge acquisition, reflective interpretation and learning.

1 Introduction

A major sea change facing all organisations at present is the accelerated globalisation of competition and the gradual redistribution of economic activity from manufacturing to services, particularly in most developed economies (Ettlie and Rosenthal, 2011). These macro trends, which follow closely many of Gershuny's (1978) predictions regarding the service dominated nature of post industrial societies, illustrate the emergence of a newly reconstituted competitive arena in which many of the rules and rewards of the past have changed (Arrow, 1983). Illustrating this shift, Ng, Maull and Smith (2009) found that even traditional manufacturing companies now often generate the majority of their revenues from services. de Jong et al (2003) have argued that this means that all firms are now service firms to some extent and that service research has not kept up with the demands of economic reality (Ng et al, 2009). Gronroos (2001) has called for more research that will enable organisations in this new service era to function more effectively and productively. In response, researchers have shown a growing interest in service innovation with initial insights emerging (Fuglsang, 2002). But to date there has been a collective struggle to comprehensively capture what this new combination of terminology actually means (Chase and Garvin, 1989; de Jong et al, 2003; Lovelock and Gummesson, 2004). Flint et al (2005) have argued that despite best efforts and achievements to date, little is known about whether service innovation is purposeful, ad hoc, informal or spontaneous. Spohrer and Maglio (2008) concluded that the service innovation concept remains theoretically problematic.

It is in the spirit and tradition of seeking conceptual validation that this paper takes a step back and asks two overarching questions, what is service innovation, and how does it occur? By drawing upon the concepts of market relations and organisational learning, we explore the process of how service innovations are generated and developed. In dealing with our research questions, a conceptual view of service innovation is offered based on what we see as an active and reflective learning process. This work offers the view that service innovations are constructed and reconstructed based on active interpretation and learning. We demonstrate that service innovation occurs because organisations invest in 'knowing' and 'reknowing' their environments in a way which facilitates constant comparison, reinterpretation and recombination. The contribution of this paper is in developing and testing a number of theoretical propositions regarding the nature of service innovation. The paper proceeds as follows. First, we explore the relationship between entrepreneurial organisations and innovation. Second, we highlight the distinctions between services and products. Thirdly, we discuss the usefulness of the 'learning' concept to understand service innovation. Our research is then presented followed by a discussion and conclusion.

2 Background

Addressing questions relating to the nature of service innovation can be elusive. Terms can be confusing, and meanings can be unclear due to the interdisciplinary nature of emerging research. For example the term service and services, in particular, are used to refer to a large range of phenomena like buying a haircut, sending a parcel or renting a hire car (Ng et al, 2009; Miles, 2007; Berry et al, 2006). Similarly, conceptualisations surrounding innovation, such as life cycle models, are subject to multiple definitions and ambiguity (Utterback and Abernathy, 1975). Therefore it is essential that we establish our key terms and the conceptual bounds of our contribution.

3 Entrepreneurial Organisation and Innovation

Since Schumpeter's (1934) seminal theory of economic development, researchers from across the social sciences have drawn a link between entrepreneurship and innovation (Freel, 2000). At the most extreme Hagedoorn (1996, p.884) argued that entrepreneurship *"is the personification of innovation."* According to Van de Ven (1986, p.591), each innovation is an *"idea ... may be a recombination of old ideas, a scheme that challenges the present order, a formula, or a unique approach which is perceived as new."* According to this largely Schumpeterian view, each 'new combination' contributes to ongoing waves of creative destruction, whereby entrepreneurial forms of organisation destroy and reconfigure previously dominant orders (Mishra and Zachary, 2011). Flint et al (2005) concluded that innovation does not need to be ground breakingly new to the world, just new in the eye of the beholder.

Despite the diversity of opinion regarding how entrepreneurship should be defined (Brazeal and Herbert, 1999); the trend has been for researchers to err on the side of a broader interpretation. These expanded definitions have more recently referred to innovation by entrepreneurial firms as a much more complex, dynamic and interactive social as well as economic process (Sorenson, Mattsson and Sundbo, 2010). This view stresses interactions and reflexivity between organisational members as much as the innovations themselves. According to Flint et al (2005, p.115), *"innovation is inspired by [organisational] actors responding to and interpreting a dynamic environment, continuously reflecting on their interpretations, the interpretations of others, and responses by others to their actions (i.e. innovations)."* This shift from linear to process interpretations of innovation can be seen in Van de Meer's (2007, p.192) definition that; *"Innovation is the total set of activities leading to the introduction of something new, resulting in strengthening the defendable competitive advantage of a company."* Within the paradigmatic trends outlined above, it is possible to witness a shift towards a more open and system level view which is now understood as profoundly social and embedded in ongoing structures of institutional, political and social context (Anderson, Park and Jack, 2007). According to Kalantaridis and Bika (2011), these contextual specificities give rise to unique sets of rules and conventions, as well as norms which influence competitive behaviour. Within what is now widely understood as open innovation infrastructures, contributors have referred to the 'ideas' recognised by Van de Ven (1996) coming together from many sources including users, suppliers, competitors or business service firms (Chesbrough, 2003). The dominant view of innovation at present would seem to revolve around recognising its individually strategic and participative nature while also appreciating that it takes place and is contextualised within sets of complex and open processes involving many actors (Zheng, 2010). It is against this theoretical backdrop that we now discuss the specificities of services and innovation.

4 Services and Innovation

The differences between services and physical products have been debated at length in the management and industrial marketing literatures (Araujo and Spring, 2006). At a general level, services can be defined by what Fisk, Brown and Bitner (1993) have termed their intangibility, the inseparability of their production and consumption, and their heterogeneity and perishability. Kotler (1994) argued that *intangibility* is the single feature common to all services. Because of the absence of a physical product there is no explicit transfer of ownership, and customers must place trust in the service provider (de Jong et al, 2003). This has led to a growing consensus that services are performances involving a shared interaction, even a social relationship between service providers and consumers. In this sense services can be described as *inseparable* and *simultaneous*. This means that they are produced and consumed in their performance and so require substantial interaction and mutual attention between producer and consumer (Cooper and De Brentani, 1991). Services have also been described by the extent of their *variability* and *heterogeneity* (Araujo and Spring, 2006). In this sense, no two deliveries of the same service are identical (Kotler, 1994). Bitner et al (2008) have distinguished these differences in terms of 'high tech' and 'high touch' customer-provider interactions which they see leading to 'moments of truth' where customers experience and appreciate the value of a service. Finally, services have been described as *perishable,* in that if they are not being consumed they cannot be stored. So services are not standardised widgets in the manufacturing sense, and their non standardised process nature requires that we seek ways to conceptualise their innovation in terms of organisations and entrepreneurship.Table 1 provides an illustration of the main differences between innovation in services and manufacturing as it appears in the literature.

Table 1: Differences between innovation in services and manufacturing

Source	Differences with manufacturing
Araujo and Spring (2006)	Service innovations do not require much R&D. Service firms tend to invest less in fixed assets to support innovations. Service firms spend less money on buying patents and licences.
Barras (1986)	In the service sector a lower percentage of revenues are invested in innovation. Service innovations are notoriously hard to protect and open to imitation.
De Brentani (1989)	Service innovations are easier to imitate. An explicit human resource strategy has a larger influence on the success of new services than on new manufactured products.
Den Hertog (2000)	Technology is less important for new service development.
OECD (2000)	Service innovation is not limited to changes in the product's

Source	Differences with manufacturing
	characteristics. It usually involves changes in the delivery process and client interface as well.
Sirilli and Evangelista (1998)	A lack of well educated co-workers is a main barrier to innovation in service firms, more often than in manufacturing. Organisational problems often prevent new services from being successful; organisational aspects fulfil a key role.

Adapted from de Jong et al (2003)

So services can be seen as a much closer and complex 'dance' of provider and customer than in a traditional manufacturing setting. In this sense, service innovation can essentially be seen as creating, managing and improving what is the customer's 'experience' of being part of a value creation process through their participation in a service event. Chesbrough (2003) has argued that while service innovations can be categorised by their source and driving force, eventually entrepreneurs are motivated by a need to remain profitable (Johne and Storey, 1998). This would suggest that service innovations arise as organisations strive to understand and meet customer needs, and act on these understandings. It is within the framework of markets and customer value that we address the competitive orientation of service innovators.

5 Markets, Customers and Value

Flint et al (2005) have argued that market orientation refers to the behaviour and attitude of an entire organisation. A strong market focus has been argued to manifest itself in the behaviour of organisations and their members as they generate, analyse and respond to what Jaworski and Kohli (1993) label as intelligence, or understanding. This generation of 'understanding', has been described as a complex process of sense making. In the words of Flint et al (2005, p.116) managers and organisations; *"attempt to make sense of their dynamic market environment through processes such as brainstorming exercises, competitive product analysis, trend analysis, scenario exercises, and direct customer input where they reflect on their insights and past attempts to respond to similar situations, and negotiate interpretations and responses such as innovation ideas."* It is within this complex set of activities that researchers have recognised a prominent focus on customer value perception and creation. So the activities outlined above can be understood as attempts to understand the multifaceted nature of customer value perception. Researchers in the field of industrial marketing have argued that what customers value changes over time, and that attention to these trends provides opportunities to stay up to date with current and changing customer value perceptions (Flint and Mentzer, 2000; Flint, Woodruff and Gardial, 2002; Woodruff and Gardial, 1996). According to these authors, service innovation requires that information relating to what customers value needs to be drawn together in a way which provides a holistic picture of overall customer needs. It is within this customer focused context that research has highlighted a learning orientation, or a desire and process for collecting and acting on insights and understandings. This is increasingly understood as falling within the conceptual boundary of organisational learning.

6 Organisational Learning

Boulding (1956) came to the conclusion that business organisations, even small ones are highly complex interpretive systems which make sense of their environments. Influenced by the work of Daft and Weick (1984) in organisational learning and Cope (2005) in entrepreneurial learning, service innovation can be interpreted as an adaptive learning process whereby organisations, guided by entrepreneurs and managers develop a body of knowledge (Blazevic and Lievens, 2004; Flint et al, 2005). From a review of the organisational learning literature we draw here upon the concepts of information and knowledge *acquisition* and *interpretation* as well as *learning* to capture the practice and process of innovation in the absence of a tangible product. According to Blazevic and Lievens (2004), the internalisation and combination of new and existing knowledge is central to the realisation of new service offerings (Huber, 1991). The dominant view within the organisational learning literature, and the one adopted here is that knowledge is acquired, interpreted and acted upon by members of a firm as a means of remaining competitive.

Acquisition refers to the process by which information is sought and obtained. According to Kogut and Zander (1992), information can come from anywhere, and can be generated directly from experiences, or vicariously from the observation of others as well as from the existing knowledge contained within the organisation (Blazevic and Lievens, 2004; Schein, 1993). Within the acquisition metaphor, information from the outside environment is combined with existing knowledge, with some organisations being better at this than others. The terms, combinative capacity (Kogut and Zander, 1992), organisational memory (Huber, 1991) and absorbtive capacity (Cohen and Levinthal, 1990) are often associated with this acquisition –

combination process. Drawing on the original literature, the notion of an interpretation stage can be understood as a process of collective reflection whereby information is given meaning (Duncan and Weiss, 1979; Hedberg, 1981; Weick, 1979). According to this view, interpretation provides the basis for organisational learning to happen. This is because it facilitates the achievement of consensus on what information actually means and the possible consequences of its use (Easterby-Smith, 1997). The third stage of Daft and Weick's (1984) model is *learning,* which they distinguish from interpretation by the inclusion of action. According to this view, learning involves an updated response or action based on the results of interpretation (Argyris and Schon, 1978; Cope, 2005). It is at this stage that new knowledge relating to the relationship between actions and consequences emerge, and new cognitive theories are formed by managers, entrepreneurs and organisations. Accordi ng to Cope (2005), individuals and organisations enter a cycle whereby learning provides new data and experiences for further reflection and interpretation. The three stages are interconnected through a feedback loop.

Figure 1: Relationships among information Acquisition, Interpretation and Learning

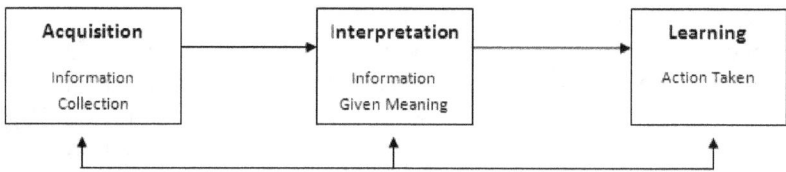

(Adapted from Daft and Weick, 1984)

So it would seem that service innovation might usefully be understood through a learning lens. But what seems central to this process is the interpretation and arrival at an informed consensus on the meaning and consequences of change (Easterby-Smith, 1997). It is this consensus which is recognised as forming the platform on which new ways of doing things are formed. In this way service innovation requires a confrontation and reinterpretation of existing conditions and practices, and the achievement of enhanced service delivery. Each newly refreshed consensus, it would seem, represents a renegotiation of the innovation stance of the organisation. Figure 1 then serves two purposes, first it underpins the view that interpretation precedes and informs innovative actions, and secondly it provides an appreciation of service innovation as the applied practice of internalised and shared understandings. Table 3 provides a summary of key themes identified in the literature.

Table 3: Key Themes in the Literature

Research	Themes	Key Contributors
Innovations	are ideas perceived as new by stakeholders; are complex, dynamic and interactive processes; are interpreted responses to a dynamic environment; are a response to market intelligence;	Van de Ven (1986) Sorenson et al (2010) Flint et al (2005) Rogers (1995)
Services	are intangible, inseparable & simultaneous; are performances where value is co-created;	Kotler (1994) Araujo and Spring (2006)
Service Innovations	are hard to protect and open to imitation; usually involve changes in the delivery process; are less likely to receive financial investment;	Barras (1986) OECD (2000) de Bretani (1989)
Markets & Customers	Market orientation refers to behaviour and attitude; Organisations make sense of market environments;	Flint and Mentzer (2000) Jaworski and Kohli (1993)
Organisational Learning	is an adaptive process of knowledge development; involves knowledge acquisition, interpretation and learning; involves the arrival at an informed organisational consensus; involves the construction of shared cognitive maps;	Shivastrava (2004) Daft and Weick (1984) Easterby-Smith (1997) Levitt and March (1988)

7 Entrepreneurial Reinterpretation and Service Innovation

Using the framework of organisational learning as understood by Daft and Weick (1984), service innovation can be understood as an outcome of critical or transformative interpretive learning (Cope, 2003). Building on the thinking of Flint et al (2005), it would seem that service innovation involves a sequence of learning activities that begins with a disorienting dilemma

and concludes with a reinterpretation of purpose and intent. We thus state that:
- Proposition 1: Service innovation is a form of entrepreneurial behaviour influenced by the interaction of the firm, its customers and its environment, and is characterised by active reinterpretation

Building upon Chesbrough's (2003) view that service innovations are motivated by a desire to remain profitable, and Johne and Storey's finding that entrepreneurs strive to understand customer needs and act upon opportunities to better serve these, we thus state that:
- Proposition 2: Reinterpreted service practices may give rise to direct and indirect performance benefits.

8 The Research

In understanding the characteristics of service innovation, this article is based on qualitative research into the lived experiences of entrepreneurial organisations who took part in doctoral research carried out by McKeever (2010). In particular it focuses on the experiences of one organisation which had been taken over and its future reinvigorated through an explicit focus on services. Since the aim of the present study is not to generalise, but to explore the nature of service innovation as a phenomenon, this approach seemed appropriate. The Logek Company was chosen because of its turbulent history and subsequent revival made it a rich case to explore (Korsgaard and Anderson, 2011).

8.1 Data Collection and Analysis

The principal data collection was through phenomenological interviews (Thompson et al, 1989; Cope, 2005). The long interview technique (McCracken, 1988) was used to take a grand tour of the topic under investigation, where the content and form of the emerging data determined the direction of interviews. The aim was to explore in some depth an entrepreneur orchestrating service innovation and how this contributed to business success. Three in-depth interview sessions were conducted and which lasted between 1 ½ and 3 hours. In all 6 hours of interview data was collected. Data was analysed through a process of coding and used to inform subsequent interviews. Data was collected to a point of theoretical saturation where conceptual categories and their contents were pursued to exhaustion. The approach used to analyse the data involved coding it, identifying concepts and highlighting their constituent sub categories. This meant reading and re-reading interview material, revisiting notes and material generated. In essence, this took the form of looking at the data and asking ourselves, "what is going on here?" This involved the constant comparative method (Glaser and Strauss, 1967; Silverman, 2000) and an iterative reviewing of the data with emerging categories and concepts. This has become an accepted approach and one reported in previous work (Human and Provan, 1997; Jack, 2005).

Table 2: Logek in Context

Name	Nature of Business	Employees	Established	Background
Bill	Logistics and freight forwarding	145	37 years	Established shortly after the discovery of North Sea oil by a local consortium. Was floated on the London stock exchange. It went through several mergers and acquisitions before being acquired privately.

9 Understanding Service Innovation

In this section a discussion of data and findings from the study are presented around three main themes emerging from the Logek case; 1) Context and circumstance; 2) Process improvements, and 3) Synergies, new markets and recombinations

9.1 Context and Circumstance

Having not used the term service innovation in interviews, but stated an interest in the Logek revival Bill began by contextualising himself and the firm. He told us, *"I've been involved in this part of the industry for twenty odd years. I transferred from one business to another until this opportunity arose... the market is in decline..... it [the company] had a series of kicking's and morale was extremely low."* This comment led to an appreciation that for Bill, the context and environment in which the firm was operating was influencing the options available. When asked about the people in the firm, he explained that in his case, *"I told them we are in a position and we have to get out of it. There's a thing around context and circumstance."* These conversations led to an appreciation that Bill understood the wider context in which Logek was situated, and had posed this as a reinterpretation challenge. He told us, *"You have to energise your people when things are bad. To display that you know what you are talking about."* This contextualisation provided an appreciation that external pressures had created a pressure on the firm in which innovation and entrepreneurial renewal were required in order to survive. This was in keeping with the findings of Johne and Storey (1998) relating to an entrepreneurial focus to remain or regain profitability. Bill explained the need to remain focused on the combination and application of knowledge; *"It's very much what you carry between your ears and to exploit that. We are looking for areas where there is a synergy."* This section has highlighted some of the antecedent pressures and forces to innovate identified by Blazevic and Lievens (2004). In this sense then, Bill was problematising the company's situation and driving a 'reinterpretation'.

9.2 Process Improvements

Leading on from discussions around renewed customer focus, Bill explained that a key outcome of this was a series of process improvements within the parameters of existing contracts. Bill explained; *"Everything nowadays goes out to tender. The only way you can make a contract more lucrative is to seriously add value, bring more to the party...do something different."* When asked for an example of how this worked, he explained; *"We managed to shave ten days off the process time on an invoice. It only took us about a day and a half's effort to do it. No-one else had done it before. We said we think we can do more for you and are you interested in working with us?"* This provided an appreciation of the enactment and discovery described by Daft and Weick (1984), and demonstrated a reinterpretation of existing practices aimed at strengthening and developing closer market relations. Bill used the phrase *"getting more business out of the same customer"* to describe this practice.

He explained that part of this was developing a relationship with what he called his *"counterpart"* in the client firm; *"The relationship at that level is extremely important. You have to be able to communicate very clearly what it is you are going to do and why you are going to do it."* So if shortening a process time by studying and understanding the needs of existing customers was a service innovation, it also set in motion a cycle of expectation. The closeness which emerged through these acts of improvement seemed to demonstrate the development of social capital and an attempt to strengthen and insulate relationships. However, these relationships and process improvements were all underpinned by a desire to remain profitable. When asked about the role of the customer in he told us; *"Ultimately their side of the bargain, in return for all we do for them is to pay their side of the bills. So that's the final judgement."* These views pointed to incremental service improvements being governed by a mix of social and economic concerns (Anderson and Jack, 2002). However, what seemed to drive more revolutionary service innovation within the broader context was that the North Sea oil and gas sector was seen to be in terminal decline. These conversations drew attention to what we saw as macro level recombinations in the Schumpeterian (1934) sense as Logek and the UK oil and gas sector entered a new period of restructuring.

9.3   Synergies, New Markets and Recombinations

Bill explained that since taking over, as well as focusing on incremental improvements in how they served existing customers, they were looking at reconfiguring the company's position in the wider market. Bill used the phrase *"the market is on the move"* to describe this macro process. In a statement which seemed to capture the fluidity of this wider innovation process, he told us; *"Twelve months ago we were operating in a single service manner. Now we probably have got about eight. Now we will probably refine that over the next three years down to about five. And one of the ones that we drop may be the one we were in a year ago."* When asked about this restructuring and the companies plans to operate in overseas markets, Bill warned that this was not a simplistic exercise, he told us that; *"We are looking for areas where there is a synergy with other sectors. Is this what they do? Can we apply our know-how there? Can we add value to that? That's expensive in terms of time, because you really have to understand what you are going into."* This statement again refers to active investments in understanding and interpretation of the external environment. It became apparent that a key currency in this process was time, and spending it studying and understanding the technical as well as the social and cultural complexities of new opportunities.

When asked for an example of these complexities and potential barriers, Bill alluded to some of the issues which can constrain efforts to take their specialist services, knowledge and expertise into new markets. He told us; *"Mexico for example is a big area of interest for oil based companies right now. Mexico is quite inefficient because they use way more people than they should. You don't go in to a state run company and say we are going to reduce jobs anywhere in the world. But that's what some people are doing.*" These views highlighted the social and cultural issues involved in bringing together information and knowledge from different contexts.

When asked how these problems were overcome, Bill explained that *"So you are getting this phenomenon within the logistics industry where there is a whole new tier of contracts appearing. We have cultivated some of these engineering contractors and you get a better deal out of them."* In many ways this new tier of contracts seemed to have created a habitus, or conceptual space which provided grounds for reinterpreting and renegotiating a new set of rules for a new context. What was particularly interesting was that the previously mentioned innovation of shaving the processing time of a contract would have been wholly inappropriate in a Mexican context. So in this section we have tried to demonstrate the interpreted and negotiated way in which Bill saw the development of new service combinations to suit overseas markets.

10 Discussion and Conclusion

Taking a customer focused and learning perspective has helped us generate a deeper appreciation of the dynamic process through which service innovations can be seen as the outcomes of reinterpreted practices. Appreciating that innovation is increasingly seen as being influenced by the wider environment in which organisations are immersed, such a perspective seems appropriate. From the experiences and examples provided by the entrepreneur, it would seem that Logek was going through a process of active learning and reinterpretation at two levels. The first was with regard to its relationship with individual clients, the second was its location and position within the overall structure of the industry. Through our conceptualisation, we have shown that service innovation, as a manifestation of an entrepreneurial orientation can impact on the performance and profitability. The direct benefits highlighted revolved around generating more revenue from existing customers and seeking out new applications for existing knowledge. The indirect benefits revolved around the strengthening of personal and business relationships, the generation of social capital, and the development of a more optimistic view of the future. In the case of Logek, this process seemed to revolve around a sterner focus on understanding 'contextual events', 'external synergies and revenue', 'organisational learning' and the maintenance of an 'internal consensus'.

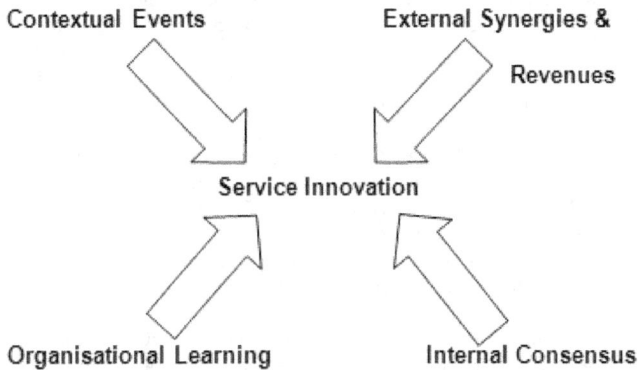

Figure 1: Service innovation process

Research in management and entrepreneurship often fails to reflect the full extent to which reflective interpretation impacts on the behaviour of organisations (Cope, 2003; 2005). Addressing our research question has highlighted the importance of viewing service innovation as a complex process involving whole organisations, the entrepreneurs and teams governing them, and the environments in which they are operating. Shane and Venkataraman (2000) have argued that this process perspective of innovation and entrepreneurship provides greater opportunities for researchers to explore "how, by whom and with what effects opportunities to create future goods and services are discovered, evaluated and exploited" (p.218). If service innovation is an active outcome of entrepreneurship, then the notion of reinterpretation of customer needs and environmental context needs more attention because it helps us to understand how service innovations move from being ideas to being driven by motivated actions. We call for more research into the role of the entrepreneur in all this, and their connections as a way of further understanding the role of the social in influencing the ambition, scale and nature of service innovations.

References:

Aldrich, H. (1979), Organisations and Environments, Englewood Cliffs, N.J. Prentice-Hall

Aldrich, H. and Martinez, M. (2001), Many are called but few are chosen: an evolutionary perspective for the study of entrepreneurship, Entrepreneurship Theory and Practice, 25(4), 41-56

Anderson, A.R. and Jack, S.L. (2002), The Articulation of Social Capital in Entrepreneurial Networks: A Glue or a Lubricant?" Entrepreneurship and Regional Development, 14, pp.193-210

Anderson, A.R., Park, J. and Jack, S. (2007), Entrepreneurial social capital; conceptualising social capital in new high-tech firms, International Small Business Journal, 25(3), pp.243-267

Araujo, L. and Spring, M. (2006), Services, products, and the institutional structure of production, Industrial Marketing Management, 35, pp.797-805

Arrow, K. J., 1983, "Innovation in large and small firms", in Ronen, J., ed., Entrepreneurship, Lexington books, Lexington MA

Barras, R. (1986), Towards a theory of innovation in services, Research Policy, 15, pp.161-173

Baumol, W. (1996), Entrepreneurship, management, and the structure of payoffs, Cambridge, MA: MIT Press.

Berry, L., Shankar, V., Parish, J.T., Cadwallader, S. and Dotzel, T. (2006), Creating new markets through service innovation, MIT Sloan Management Review, 47(2), 56-63

Bitner, M., Ostrom, A. and Morgan, F. (2008), Service blueprinting: a practical technique for service innovation, California Management Review, 50(3), pp.66-94

Blazevic, V. and Lievens, A. (2004), Learning during the new financial service innovation process antecedents and performance effects, Journal of Business Research, 57, 374-391

Boulding, K.E. (1956), General systems theory: the skeleton of a science, Management Science, 2, pp.197-207

Brazeal, D. and Herbert, T. (1999), The genesis of entrepreneurship, Entrepreneurship, Theory and Practice, 23(3), pp.29-46

Chesbrough, H. (2003), Open innovation: The new imperative for creating and profiting from technology, Harvard Business School Press, Boston

Cooper, R.G. and de Bretani, U. (1991), New industrial financial services: what distinguishes the winners, Journal of Product Innovation Management, 8(2), pp.75-91

Cope, J. (2005), Researching entrepreneurship through phenomenological inquiry: philosophical and methodological issues", International Small Business Journal, 23(2), pp. 163-189

Daft, R. and Weick, K. (1984), Toward a model of organisations as interpretation systems, The Academy of Management Review, 9(2), pp.284-295

De Brentani, U. (2001), Innovative versus incremental new business services: different keys to achieving success, Journal of Product Innovation Management, 18(3), pp.169-187

De Brentani, U. (1989), Success and failure in new industrial services, Journal of Product Innovation Management, 6, pp.239-258

De Jong, J., Vermeulen, P. (2003) Organizing successful new service development: a literature review, Management Decision, 41 (9), pp.844 – 858

Den Hertog, P. (2000), Knowledge-intensive business services as co-producers of innovation, International Journal of Innovation Management, 4(4), pp.491-528

Ettlie, J. and Rosenthal, S. (2011), Service versus manufacturing innovation, Journal of Production Innovation Management, 28(2), pp.285-299

Fisk, R., Brown, S. and Bitner, M.J. (1993), Tracking the evolution of the services marketing literature, Journal of Retailing, 69(1), pp.61-105

Francis, D, and Sandberg, W. (2000), Friendship within entrepreneurial teams and its association with team and venture performance, Entrepreneurship Theory and Practice, 25, pp.235-247

Freel, M. (2000), Barriers to product innovation in small manufacturing firms, International Small Business Journal, 18(2), pp.60-80

Leading Issues in Innovation Research

Froehle, C. and Roth, A. (2007), A resource-process framework of new service development, Productions and Operations Management, 16(2), pp.169-188

Gershuny, J. (1978), After Industrial Society: The Emerging Self-Service Economy, Macmillan London

Glaser, B. and Strauss, A. (1967), The discovery of grounded theory, de Gruyter, New York

Gronroos, C. (2001), The perceived service quality concept – a mistake, Managing Service Quality, 11(3), 150-152

Hagedoorn, J. (1996), Innovation and Entrepreneurship: Schumpeter Revisited, Industrial and Corporate Change, 5 (3), pp.883-896

Huber, G.P. (1991), Organisational learning: the contributing process and the literature, Journal of Business Research, 40, pp.99-111

Hult, G. and Ferrell, O. (1997), a global learning organisation structure and market information processing, Journal of Business Research, 40, 155-166

Johne, A. and Storey, C. (1998), new service development: a review of the literature and annotated bibliography, European Journal of Marketing, 3(1), pp.184-252

Kalantaridis, C. and Bika, Z. (2011), Entrepreneurial origin and the configuration of innovation in rural areas: the case of Cumbria, North West England, Environment and Planning A, 43, pp.866-884

Kelly, D. and Storey, C. (2000), New service development: initiation strategies, International Journal of Service Industry Management, 11(1), pp.45-63

Korsgaard, S. and Anderson, A. (2011), Enacting entrepreneurship as social value creation, International Small Business Journal, 29(2), pp.135-151

Kotler, P. (1994), Marketing management: analysis, planning, implementation and control, Prentice Hall International London

Lovelock, C. and Gummesson, E. (2004), Whither service marketing? In search of a new paradigm and fresh perspectives, Journal of service research, 7(1), pp.20-41

Lundvall, B. (1992), National systems of innovation: towards a theory of innovation and interactive learning, Pinter Publishers London

McCracken, G. (1988), *The Long Interview*, Newbury Park, CA: Sage Publications

Patton, M. (1990), Qualitative evaluation and research methods, Thousand Oaks, Sage

Porter, M. (1990), the competitive advantage of nations, Macmillan London

Schumpeter, J. (1934), the Theory of Economic Development, Cambridge, Harvard University Press

Shivastrava, P. (1983), A typology of organisational learning systems, Journal of Management Studies, 20(1), pp.7-28

Silverman, D. (Ed), 2000, *Doing Qualitative Research: A Practical Handbook*, Sage, London

Sirilli, G. and Evangelista, R. (1998), Technological innovation in services and manufacturing; results from an Italian study, Research Policy, 27, pp.881-899

Sorenson, F., Mattesson, J. and Sundbo, J. (2010), Experimental methods in innovation research, Research Policy, 39, pp.313-322

Spohrer, P. and Maglio, J. (2008), Fundamentals of service science, Journal of the Academy of Marketing Science, 36(1), pp.18-20

Swedberg, R. (2000), Entrepreneurship: A Social Science View, (ed), Oxford University Press

Utterback, J. and Abernathy, W. (1985), A dynamic model of process and product innovation, Omega, 3(6), pp.639-656

Van de Meer, H. (2007), Open innovation – the Dutch treat: challenges in thinking in business models, Creativity and Innovation Management, 16(2), pp.192-202

Van de Ven, A. (1986), Central problems in the management of innovation, Management Science, 32(5), Organisation Design, pp.590-605.

Edward McKeever, Sarah Jack and Danny Soetanto

Catalysts and Barriers of Open Innovation for SMEs in Transition Economy

Allan Lahi and Tiit Elenurm
Estonian Business School, Tallinn, Estonia
Originally published in The Proceedings of ICIE 2014

Editorial commentary
As Lahi and Elenurm note, discussions on open innovation have often tended to focus on large organisations. By contrast, these authors consider how smaller enterprises can be encouraged to participate in open innovation activity. They suggest that economic benefits can be realised from such participation. In this empirical study, Lahi and Elenurm compared and contrasted views on, and perceptions of, open innovation in SMEs in transition and more industrialised economies.

Some points for discussion, learning and reflection arising from this paper include:
- The internal and external factors that influence participation in open innovation.
- The importance of access to external resources for open innovation in SMEs.
- The role of network development for open innovation.
- Open innovation and intellectual property.
- Impact of owner-manager characteristics on open innovation.
- The characteristics of an open innovation leader.

Abstract: Most open innovation studies have focused on different natures of innovation and innovation processes that generally take place in large enterprises. Whereas, there is no evidence that open innovation is more inherent to large enterprises rather than to SME-s. On the contrary, smaller enterprises could be more flexible to explore new business ideas. The present qualitative study of open innovation focuses on open innovation impact and success factors for SME-s. The aim of this research is to create qualitative basis to following quantitative research within

SME-s and find answers to the research questions: how to do encourage the open innovation for smaller enterprises? What could be the main implicating factors to pay attention? The research has been provided on the basis of questionnaires and following expert interviews. Three countries were selected. Estonia represents a transition country from efficiency-driven to innovation–driven economy. Sweden is an innovation leader country from similar Northern European cultural background to Estonia. United Kingdom represents a large industrialized country with innovation-driven economy in Western Europe. Experts were selected from industry (SME representatives), academy and business consultants from each of the three countries. The questionnaire was constructed for balanced evaluation of internal and external factors that have impact to open innovation process. Factors were presented from literature study and interviewees had freedom to add factors that were important by their opinion but were missed out from proposed questions. The interviews were conducted face-to-face or by phone conference. The interviewees were asked to indicate five most important factors of open innovation and combine them with forces that have biggest impact to their reveal evidence. Finally interviewees were asked to rank up to ten supportive and prohibitive forces. Several open innovation success factors have dual characteristic simultaneously – prohibitive and supportive. The main factors that influence the process of open innovation are the commercialisation of open innovation, the link between the innovation process and the market, and the SME´s senior management´s motivation and ability to learn. Most experts identified personal qualities of the open innovation leader as a critical factor to a successful open innovation process, where the success will be measured by commercialisation of open innovation results. The main differences between transition and innovation-driven economies were identified in the field of intellectual property commercialisation. There is also contradiction between "Experience of utilization of external knowledge" and "Involvement or employees to innovation processes" that is evaluated high in transition economy and lower in innovation-driven economies. In the future research these questions will need to be clarified to determine the more important.. Experts did not have common view about importance of the intellectual property commercialization capability for open innovation.

Keywords: open innovation, SME, impact factors, transition economy

1 Introduction

According to traditional approach, innovation has been interpreted as process inside a single organisation that is focused on gaining competitive advantage at the marketplace. When trying to understand traditional (closed) innovation that takes place inside one organisation, many innovation studies have focused on large companies with internal R&D laboratories and capabilities to discover, develop and commercialize technologies

(Chesbrough, 2003). Participation in formal and informal entrepreneurial networks has been discussed as a factor of successful innovative entrepreneurship since 1980th years (Breschi and Malerba, 2005). Increasing mobility of knowledge workers, rapid development of internet based knowledge networks and expansive scopes of possible external suppliers have undermined the effectiveness of traditional innovation system (Chesbrough, 2003). Open Innovation (OI) is defined by Chesbrough as „the use of purposive Inflows and outflows of knowledge to accelerate internal innovation, and to expand the markets for external use of innovation, respectively" (Chesbrough, 2003). The assumption for open innovation is readiness of the organisations to commercialize not only internal ideas, but also ideas outside the organisation, as well as commercialize their ideas through external channels. At the same time open innovation assumes disclosure of some business information to outsiders in order to have their meaningful contribution.

Most open innovation studies have focused on different natures of innovation and innovation processes that generally take place in large enterprises (Chesborough 2010). There is no qualitative evidence that would demonstrate significant advantage of larger enterprises in innovation. Smaller enterprises are often more flexible to discover new business opportunities and that could be an advantage for the innovation process management that utilizes radically new ideas. McMullen et al. (2007) explain that an entrepreneurial opportunity can be either an objective construct visible to an entrepreneur or a new innovative construct created by a knowledgeable entrepreneur. However, only few of smaller enterprises have sufficient capacity to manage the whole innovation process by themselves and this encourages them from innovation cooperation with other enterprises (Edwards et al. 2005). Small technology firms have an important role on revitalizing economy but they face infrastructural, marketing, financing and internationalisation challenges in their business development (Pellikka and Virtanen, 2009). Encouragement of SMEs could be a key factor for development of the economy on local, regional and national levels (Jones, O.; Tilley, F., 2003). The main research question is, how to encourage the open onnovation for smaller enterprises. What are the key catalysts and barriers of OI for SME in more and less advanced market economies? How business and institutional environment impacts openness and success of innovation?

2 Literature review

2.1 General approach to impact factors in transition economies

The main areas of open innovation analysis cover various perspectives. The studies cover following areas:
- industrial dynamics of open innovation (Christensen, et al 2005);
- open innovation processes in a particular industry sector (Cooke, 2005), (Henkel, 2006) or;
- ways in which to inspire open innovation (Lichtenthaler, 2008).

Open innovation is however not a clear-cut concept. It comes in many forms and shapes which add to the richness of the concept but hinders theory development. Therefore, it is necessary to develop open innovation frameworks. Different sets of open innovation practices can be contrasted by developing matrices distinguishing various forms of open innovation. A first way of doing this is recognizing that open innovation reflects less of a dichotomy (completely open versus completely closed) than a continuum with varying degrees of openness (Dahlander and Gann, 2010).

Similarly to closed innovation, most open innovation research so far has taken place in large companies where the open innovation was first noticed as a research field. Discussions on the open innovation concept in small and medium size enterprises were excluded from mainstream (West, et al, 2006) by stating the following reasons:
- open innovation is more easily studied in larger companies because SMEs have less ability to access external resources and have smaller technological assets to knowledge exchange than larger companies (Narula, 2004);
- SMEs use external means of innovation more than large companies because they consider alliances or network as ways to extend their technological competences (Edwards et al, 2005). Therefore open innovation concept is practice familiar to the SMEs;
- SME networks are limited by subcontracting to large enterprises (Rothwell & Dodgson, 1994) or subcontracting from other SMEs (Rothwell, 1991)
- SMEs consider external sources as routes to marketing and sales channels at the later (commercialisation) stages of innovation,

while open innovation normally focuses more on the early stages of innovation, addressing external technology sourcing and networking with technology providers and innovative companies in supply chain (Vanhaverbeke & Cloodt, 2006).

It is important to study to which extent these assumptions of researchers hold in different types business environment and how internal and external factors influence OI capability of SMEs.

2.2 Internal and external factors influencing open innovation

Dahlander and Gann (2010) use the dimensions of inbound versus outbound open innovation and pecuniary versus non-pecuniary interactions. The four cells in the matrix are labelled as acquiring, sourcing, selling and revealing as shown on Figure 1 below. This model may be a good starting point for empirical research to better understand the activities comprising each of the four strategies and their effectiveness for different organizations and indifferent contexts

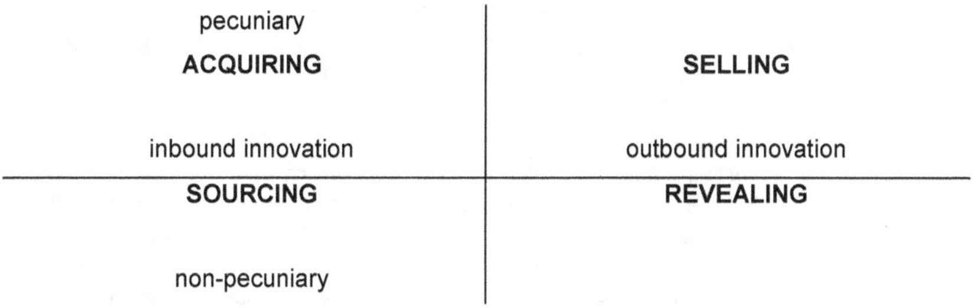

pecuniary	
ACQUIRING	SELLING
inbound innovation	outbound innovation
SOURCING	REVEALING
non-pecuniary	

Figure 1: Dimensional matrix of different innovation interactions

Detailed comparison of these four interaction types is summarized in Table 1:

Table 1: Comparison of four innovation types (Dahlander and Gann, 2010)

	Acquiring	Selling	Sourcing	Revealing
Focus	Acquiring inventions and input to the innovative process through informal and formal relationships (e.g. Chesbrough and Crowther, 2006; Christensen et al., 2005)	Out-licensing or selling products in the market place (e.g. Lichtenthaler and Ernst, 2009; Chesbrough and Rosenbloom, 2002)	Sourcing external ideas and knowledge from suppliers, customers, competitors, consultants, universities, public research organizations, etc. (e.g. Fey and Birkinshaw, 2005; Lakhani et al., 2006; Laursen and Salter, 2006a)	Revealing internal resources to the external environment (e.g. Allen, 1983; Henkel, 2006; Nuvolari, 2004; von Hippel and von Krogh, 2003)
Advantages driving openness	Gaining access to resources and knowledge of partners (Powell et al., 1996)	Commercialize products that are 'on the shelf'	Access to a wide array of ideas and knowledge (Laursen and Salter, 2006a)	Marshal resources and support (Henkel, 2006)
	Leveraging complementarities with partners (Dyer and Singh, 1998)	Outside partners may be better equipped to commercialize inventions to the mutual interests of both organizations (Chesbrough and Rosenbloom, 2002)	Discovering radical new solutions to solving problems (Lakhani et al., 2006)	Gaining legitimacy from external environment (Nuvolari, 2004)
				Foster incremental and cumulative innovation (Murray and O'Mahony, 2007; Scotchmer, 1991)

Leading Issues in Innovation Research

	Acquiring	Selling	Sourcing	Revealing
Disadvantages driving closeness	Difficult to maintain a large number of ties with different partners (Ahuja, 2000)	Over-commitment to own product and technologies make it difficult to out-license (Lichtenthaler and Ernst, 2007)	Many sources create an attention problem (Laursen and Salter, 2006a)	Difficult to capture the benefits that accrue
	Risk of outsourcing critical dimension of the firm's		Difficult to choose and combine between too many alternatives (Sapienza et al., 2004)	Internal resources can leak to competitors (Laursen and Salter, 2006b)

Catalysts and barriers of open innovation for SMEs can be different when acquiring selling, sourcing or revealing innovations depending on their business model, organizational culture available resources and networks. Earlier research that compared innovation management challenges in Estonia and in the United Kingdom (Elenurm, 2010) gave evidence that Estonian enterprises consider leveraging suppliers for ideas less important for their innovative effort that UK enterprise. The first Global Entrepreneurship Monitor study in Estonia in 2012 revealed that if early-stage entrepreneurs aim to sell their innovative products to foreign markets, they more often receive business development advice from external sources and less often from their family compared to other entrepreneurs (Arro et al. 2013).

The innovation barriers could be classified as external or internal barriers. External can be further subdivided into supply, demand and environment related. Supply barriers include difficulties in obtaining technological information, raw materials, and finance. Demand barriers are associated with customer needs, their perception of the risk of innovation, and domestic or foreign market limitations. Environmental ones include various government regulations, antitrust measures, and policy actions. Internal barriers can be further subdivided into resource related, e.g. lack of internal funds, technical expertise or management time, culture and systems related, e.g. out-of date accountancy systems (Rush and Bessant, 1992), and human nature related, e.g. attitude of top manager to risk or employee resistance to innovation.

2.2.1 External factors

Keizer et al. (2002) divide external factors into three groups:
- collaboration with other organisations;
- linkages with knowledge centres and
- utilizing financial resources or support regulations.

Entrepreneurs consider collaboration with other firms as a very important part of their innovation efforts (Massa and Testa, 2008). In particular, the work of Kaminski et al. (2008) show that collaboration with suppliers can contribute to the innovativeness of SMEs. Collaboration with suppliers may also have the goal of overcoming size constraints, while collaboration with both suppliers and customers may be performed for the purpose of co-design.

Connections with knowledge centres that include contributions by professional consultants, university researchers and technology centres have been studied by various research groups (Le Blanc et al., 1997; Hoffman et al., 1998; Oerlemans et al., 1998), as well as contribution by innovation centres and Chambers of Commerce (Oerlemans et al., 1998). Regarding variables which relate to utilizing financial resources or support regulations, availability of R&D funding was shown to be an important influencer of innovative efforts in SMEs (Le Blanc et al., 1997; Hoffman et al., 1998).

2.2.2 Internal factors

Open Innovation is based on two main pillars that could be supported or impeded by cultural norms of organisation. The first pillar is the usage of external technologies to advance internal innovation projects. While the second is the commercialisation of the innovation project results using external distribution channels. To characterize the different flow patterns, Gassmann and Enkel (2004) use the terms outside-in (integrating external knowledge, customers and suppliers, "Inbound" by Chesbrough) and inside-out (selling IP and bringing ideas to market by transferring them to the outside environment, "Outbound" by Chesbrough). Gassmann and Enkel (2004) further distinguish a third core process or archetype of Open Innovation - the coupled process. The coupled process combines "the outside-in and inside-out processes by working in alliances with complementary partners in which give and take is crucial for success". Based on their empirical research, Gassmann and Enkel conclude that although all three processes are necessary to successfully embark on an Open Innovation strategy, companies usually focus on one primary process while more or less integrating elements of the others. However, for the ease of illustration and discussion, this thesis only distinguishes between inbound and outbound processes.

3 Assumptions for expert study

The factors, having implication to Open Innovation could act at the same time as catalysts or barriers. The main factors could be summarized as descripted on Figure 2. We can assume that the factors have different exact meaning and different impact to success of Open Innovation and unfortunately **there is no finding from literature about impact of the exact factors and their dependencies.**

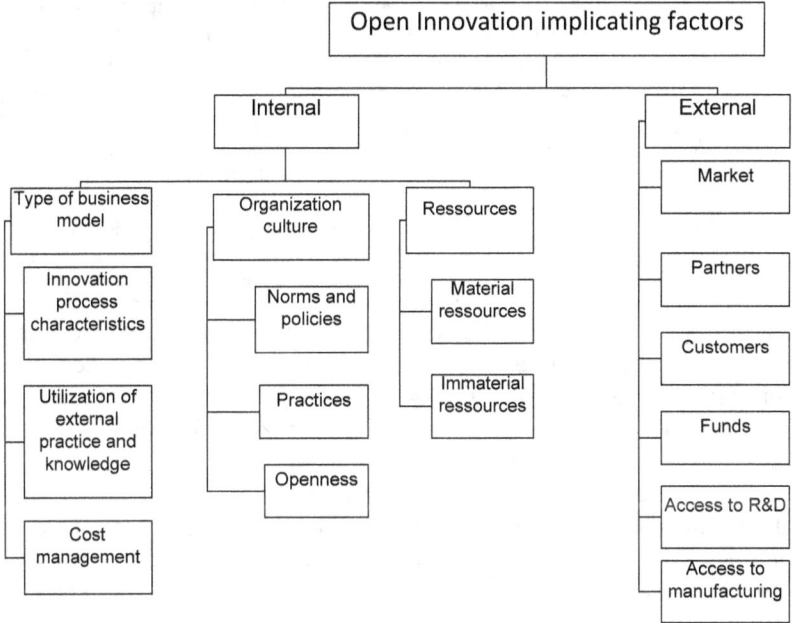

Figure 2: Factors, implicating to open innovation

4 Methodology of expert assessment

To set up further empirical research, an expert opinion questionnaire was produced and provided. The target group consists in total of 10 experienced SME representatives, researchers and business consultants with long track record on Open Innovation networks from Estonia, Sweden and the UK. SME representatives were from innovative small companies (10-49 employees) and microenterprises (start-ups) that had previous experience with commercialisation of new technology. Represented sectors were construction, materials processing and nanotechnology. Business consultants had significant track record in Open Innovation networks with participation of SMEs. The target group was selected to have variety of opinions and find factors that could have common importance to all sectors.

Table 2: Economy type and perceptions trends in entrepreneurship culture of selected countries

Country	Economy type (The Global Competitiveness Report)	Entrepreneurship culture type (Xavier, et al, 2013)
Estonia	Transition from efficiency-driven to innovation-driven economy	Nordic culture with high opportunity perceptions and low capabilities perceptions
Sweden	Innovation-driven economy	Nordic culture with high opportunity perceptions and low capabilities perceptions
United Kingdom	Innovation-driven economy	European culture with low opportunity perceptions and high capabilities perceptions

The 5 page questionnaire, based on the findings of literature study, and was constructed and presented to 4 SME experts. It was then adjusted, corrected and re-phrased according to the results of the pilot study. This procedure aimed to increase the content validity of the questionnaire. The results of pilot testing were not incorporated in the expert assessment data. The questionnaire was divided into four sections. Section A was about evaluation of internal and external factors impact to Open Innovation process. The scale was even from 1 to 10 to avoid neutral marks on centre of odd scale. Factors were presented from literature study and interviewees had freedom to add factors that were important by their opinion but missed from proposed questions.

The interviews for the questionnaire completion were face-to-face or by phone conference, since it was predicted (rightly as was later realized) that the response rate with a e-mail or postal questionnaire of such length and complexity would be unacceptably low. The interviewees were owners of companies (6), researchers (2) and business consultants (2). The study included many variables, but in the limited space of this article will focus only the main factors.

In Section B interviewees were asked to indicate five most important factors of OI and combine them with forces that have biggest impact to their reveal evidence. Two supportive forces and two prohibitive forces were asked. In Sections C and D interviewees were asked to rank up to ten supportive and prohibitive forces, listed in Section B.

As the study was qualitative and collected expert opinions from 10 people, no complex qualitative research methods were used in data processing. The results were also studied by target groups and countries.

5 Results of expert assessments

The common understanding (view) of the academy, industry and consultants was that OI is more implemented and studied in large enterprises rather than in the SME´s. Some differences origin from understanding of open innovation and measurement of innovation success. In general, the studies like Eurobarometer focus more to innovation expenditures than economic growth, generated by innovation. These differences could have some impact to expert's attitude.

5.1 Internal factors

The most important factors seem to be (with average score) as described on Table 4:

Table 3: Open innovation implication factors

	Average	Standard deviation
Internal factors		
Connection of innovation processes with market	9,8	0,422
Motivation and learning capability of senior management	9,4	0,966
Innovation process openness	9,2	0,632
Experience of utilization of external knowledge	8,8	0,789

	Average	Standard deviation
Internal factors		
Availability of technology for development	8,8	0,789
Involvement or employees to innovation processes	8,6	0,966
Availability of time, required for development	8,6	0,843
Innovation process manageability	8,2	1,317
Presence of competent employees	7,9	1,197
Openness of product and technology development	7,8	1,033
Intellectual Property (IP) and commercialisation capability	6,6	3,134
External factors		
Public Sector innovation policy	9,5	0,707
Cooperation readiness of society	9,2	0,919
Market	9,1	0,876
Partners	9	0,471
Access to external manufacturing resources	8,7	0,949

By average indicators, Intellectual Property (IP) commercialisation capability of IP got only 6.6 points with standard deviation 3,13 that shows high variety of opinions for that factor. That factor has more impact for large enterprises. One important factor that was mentioned by interviewees is learning capability of managers.

Due to the limited number of expert interviews the conclusions between factor differences between Nordic countries and the UK and also between transition and innovation-driven economies could be speculative however, need to be studied more thoroughly in the future. The main difference could be in commercialisation of IP that is evaluated low in a transition economy and high in innovation-driven economies. There is also contradiction between "Experience of utilization of external knowledge" and "Involvement or employees to innovation processes" that is evaluated high in transition economy and lower in innovation-driven economies. In the future research, these questions will need to be clarified to understand, which is more important.

Most interviewees brought out that external factors have less impact to successful OI process than internal factors. However, openness of society and Public Sector innovation policy were marked by transition economy experts as factors with extremely high influence to Open Innovation.

The most important OI factors are represented on Figure 3:

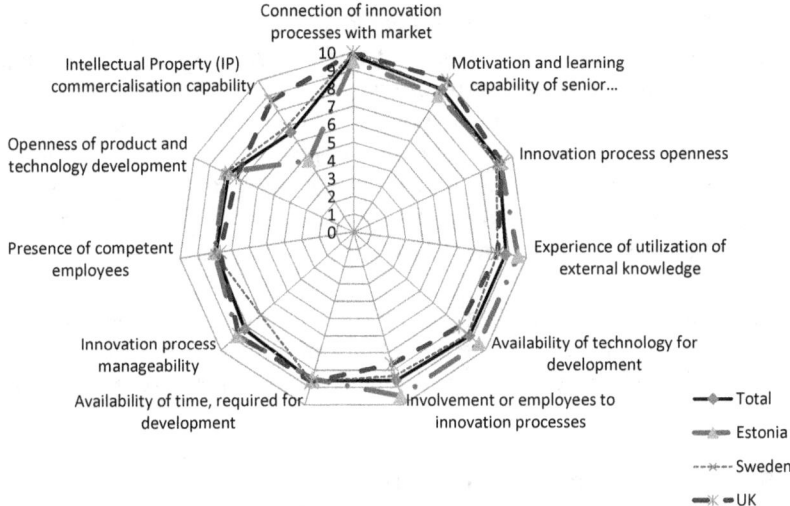

Figure 3: Variety of OI implication factors by economy type

5.1.1 The most important OI influence factors

OI landscape and feasibility study (OILFS), provided by JICS and Pera in UK on 2009, identified the 5 main OI critical factors for SME-s: Intellectual Property, cultural differences between business and academy, defining the needs for collaboration, finding the right people and trust. By our study, the main OI influence factor was proposed to be the innovation leader, manager or entrepreneur, his/her personal properties, commitment, knowledge and attitudes that could be supported or prevented by education, creativity and society's attitude. That was mentioned by all interviewees. The main difference, of OI leaders, comparing with closed innovation leaders, is readiness to share IP to build more efficient business model. Personnel properties like openness and leadership are advantages. The personal properties of OI leader and persons, involved into OI process, were highly evaluated also in OILFS study.

The second important factor was mentioned is access to human capital with appropriate attitudes. Third important factor that was mentioned is availability and quality of cooperation partners. Access to financial resources and public sector innovation policy were mentioned as most important external factors that could have significant influence to success of OI process.

In OILFS the cultural differences were identified as the most critical factor whereas in our study they were not prioritized. These differences origin from organisation reward structure types as universities are primarily oriented towards success in publishing and acquiring of grants and in the private sector the focus is on profit. The problem is that these aims are not mutually aligned and sometimes could not be mutually aligned without changing of organisation focus. On the future research, the cultural differences between organisations will have more detailed approach.

By OILFS, the main stumbling point of every OI project could be intellectual property. In our research the importance of IP and it's commercialisation was evaluated highly by UK experts and lower by experts from Sweden and Estonia.

5.2 Supporting and prohibitive forces

For OI, the same forces could be at the same time supportive or prohibitive. The main forces were mentioned:
- Leaders attitude end personal properties
- Education system an it's support to cooperation and creativity
- Availability of cooperation partners
- Cooperation experience

Leader can inspire the Open Innovation process and drive the innovation through all phases from initiation to market. Leader can also paralyse the knowledge sharing that is necessary for OI. The main personal properties are the same like for each leader and in addition leader will trust the OI network. Importance of cooperation experience could be reduced by recruiting of partner who has that kind of experience and whom the OI leader can trust.

6 Case studies

Two cases that could illustrate the findings from research are described below.

An open innovation consortium, led by R&D oriented SME Natural Resources Ltd, developed a novel environmentally friendly 3D paper packaging technology using injection moulding principles, known from plastics industry. The technology enables utilisation of post-consumer recyclable materials as raw materials, their finished product is fully recyclable and minimises the waste streams and transportation needs of materials. Consortium contained 7 partners from industry and 2 academic institutions. The leader was committed and kept the whole consortium on a clear business course. IP issues were agreed before the project starts and each participant got estimated benefits from the project. The research partners were well managed and developed technology was successfully commercialized. The key success factors were right leader, god handling of IP, selection and finding of right partners, the right R&D problem and minimization of potential cultural conflicts between industry and academy.

An Open Innovation consortium, initiated by an SME from Estonia, developed an indoor 3D navigation solution for construction industry. That solution enables accurate indoor positioning, using smartphones, tablets or other portable computing devices and real time cooperation with CAD systems. By calculations, the technology enables to reduce time waste on construction site by 50%.. Project started on 2008, on the top of economic recession and the initiator of the project lose the interest to invest time or other resources to the project. Some SME partners dropped out too. The rest of the consortium believes to success of the project and new SME partners around Europe were recruited. At the end of the project a pre-production prototype was tested and validated both in laboratory and on construction site. For successful market entry the technology needs at least additional 2 years for product development but that could not be done because of following circumstances:
- there is not clear, interested leader who can take care for commercialisation of that technology;
- for industrial partners the IP is too far from market;
- end users, that were included into development, are interested in usage of technology but not in commercialisation of that technology.

7 Conclusions and future research

Most of experts identified personal qualities of the open innovation leader as critical factor for successful open innovation process where the success will be measured by commercialisation of open innovation results.

OI could be divided into six phases:
1. Initiation
2. Motivation and capabilities involvement
3. Idea development
4. OI enablers analysis and development
5. OI environment development (external factors)
6. Monetisation and commercialisation of OI results

Qualities of the open innovation leader that contribute to these phases will be differentiated in our further research. The main attention in OI research in large organizations has been so far turned on phases 4 and 5 (the final phases) although assumption for successful OI that passes the phase 6 is start or phase 1. All interviewees agreed that main factor for successful OI is SME entrepreneur as the leader of OI and his /her attitude and personal properties.

Public sector's innovation policy is focused on innovation clusters, supportive systems and finances that are themes on phases 4 and 5. Business angels start from Phase 3. At the same time, Steve Jobs and Bill Gates, for example, started from Phase 1 without any supportive innovation system and reached phase 6. The challenge is, how to identify the potential innovations on Phase 1, select them on Phase 2 and support through Phases 3-5 to Phase 6. The future research will be focused to find an answer to that question.

Education system can support continuous learning and cooperation or support competition between individuals and individualisation.
Availability of cooperation partners is important but depends from cooperation capabilities of leader and management team. In open world, it is possible to hire cooperation partners crossing the borders of usual business region.

References

Arro, T., Elenurm, T., Küttim, M., Liigus, E., Masso, J., Mets, T., Paes, K., Raudsaar, M., Rebane, K., Reino, A., Põder, K., Venesaar, U. (2013) "Globaalne ettevõtlusmonitooring 2012. Eesti raport", [online], http://www.arengufond.ee/upload/Editor/Publikatsioonid/Arengufond%20GEM%20uuri ngu%20raport.pdf

Breschi, S. and Malerba, F. (Eds), (2005) Clusters, Networks, and Innovation. Oxford: Oxford University Press.

Chesbrough, H. (2003). Open Innovation. Boston: Harvard Business School Press.

Chesborough, H (2010) Open Innovation: A Key to Achieving Socioeconomic Evolution Economy, Culture & History JAPAN SPOTLIGHT Bimonthly, Jan/Feb 2010

Christensen, J.F.; Olsesen, M.H.; Kjær, J.S. (2005). The industrial dynamics of open innovation – evidence from the transformation of consumer electronics. Research Policy , 34, 1533-1549.

Cooke, P. (2005). Regionally asymmetric knowledge capabilities and open innovation. Research Policy , 34, 1128–1149.

Dahlander, L.,Gann,D.M.,2010. How open is innovation? Research Policy 39, 699–709

Edwards, T.; Delbridge, R.; Munday, M. (2005). Understanding innovation in small and medium-sized enterprises: a process manifest. Technovation , 25, 1119–1120.

Elenurm, T. (2010). Innovation Challenges and Opportunities in Estonian Enterprises. In: 2nd International Conference "Economies of Central and Eastern Europe: Convergence, Opportunities and Challenges". Conference Proceedings. Tallinn 13-15:, 2010.

Facilitating Open Innovation: Landscape and Feasibility Study, JISC, October 2009

Gassmann O., Enkel E., 2004, Towards a Theory of Open Innovation: Three Core Process Archetypes", R&D Management Conference.

Henkel, J. (2006). Selective revealing in open innovation processes: the case of embedded Linux. Research Policy , 35, 953–969.

Herzog, P. (2011) Open and Closed Innovation. Different Cultures for Different Strategies, 2nd revised edition

Hofstede, G., Neuijen, B., Ohayv, D. D. and Sanders, G. (1990). Measuring organizational cultures: a qualitative and quantitative study across 20 cases. Administrative Science Quarterly, 35 (2): 286-316.

Hoffman, K., Parejo, M., Bessant, J., Perren, L., 1998. Small firms, R&D technology and innovation in the UK: a literature review. Technovation 18 (1), 39–55.

Kaminski,P.C.,deOliveira,A.C.,Lopes,T.M.,2008.Knowledge transfer in product development processes: a case-study in small and medium enterprises (SMEs) of the metal-mechanic sector from Sao Paulo, Brazil. Technovation 28 (1–2), 29–36.

Keizer, J., Dijstra, L., Halman, J.I.M., 2002. Explaining innovative efforts of SMEs. An exploratory survey among SMEs in the mechanical and electrical engineering sector in The Netherlands. Technovation 22, 1–13.

Le Blanc, L.J., Nash, R., Gallagher, D., Gonda, K., Kakizaki, F., 1997. A comparison of US and Japanese technology management and innovation. International Journal of Technology Management 13 (5–6), 601–614.

Lichtenthaler, U. (2006). Leveraging knowledge assets: success factors of external technology commercialization. Wiesbaden, Betriebswirtschaftslehre für Technologie und Innovation, Vol. 53

Lichtenthaler, U., 2008. Leveraging technology assets in the presence of markets for knowledge. European Management Journal , 26, 122–134.

Lichtenthaler, U.,Lichtenthaler,E., 2009. A capability – based framework for open innovation: complementing absorptive capacity. Journal of Management Studies 46(8),1315–1338.
Lin, C., Tan, B. and Chang, S. (2002). The critical factors for technology absorptive capacity. Industrial Management + Data Systems; 102, 5/6, pp. 300–308
Massa, S., Testa, S., 2008. Innovation and SMEs: misaligned perspectives and goals among entrepreneurs, academics, and policy makers. Technovation 28 (7), 393–407.
McMullen, J.S., Plummer, L.A. and Asc, Z.J. 2007. What is entrepreneurial opportunity?", Small Business Economics, Vol 28, No. 4, pp 363-379.
Mehrwald, H. (1999). Das "Not Invented Here"-Syndrom in Forschung und Entwicklung. Wiesbaden
Narula, R. (2004). R&D collaboration by SMEs: new opportunities and limitations in the face of globalisation. Technovation , 25, 153-161.
Oerlemans, L.A.G., Meeus, M.T.H., Boekema, F.W.M., 1998. Do networks matter for innovation: the usefulness of the economic network approach in analysing innovation. Journal of Economic and Social Geography 89 (3), 298–309.
Pelikka, J and Virtanen, M. 2009. Problems of commercialization in small technology-based firms. International Journal of Entrepreneurship and Innovation Management, 9 (3), 267-284.
Rothwell, R. (1991). External networking and innovation in small and medium-sized manufacturing firms in Europe. Technovation , 11 (2), 93-112.
Rothwell, R., & Dodgson, M. (1994). Innovation and size of firm. rmt: M. Dodgson, Handbook of industrial innovation (lk 310-324). Aldershot: Edward Elgar Publishing Limited.
The Global Competitiveness Report 2010-2011, World Economic Forum, 2010
Vanhaverbeke, W., & Cloodt, M. (2006). Open innovation in value networks. rmt: H. Chesbrough, W. Vanhaverbeke, & J. West, Open Innovation: Researching a New Paradigm. NY: Oxford University Press.
Xavier, R., Kelley, D., Kew, J., Herrington, M., Vorderwülbecke, A., (2013), GEM 2012 Global Report
West, J.; Vanhaverbeke, W.; Chesbrough, H. (2006). Open innovation: a research agenda. rmt: H. Chesbrough, W. Vanhaverbeke, & J. West, Open Innovation: Researching a New Paradigm. NY: Oxford University Press.
Wind, J. and Mahajan, V. (1997). Issues and opportunities in new product development: an introduction to the special issue. Journal of Marketing Research, 34 (1): 1-12.

Strategic Creativity as a Strength in Microsized Enterprises

Tiina Tarvainen
University of Eastern Finland, Joensuu, Finland
Originally published in The Proceedings of ECIE 2011

> **Editorial commentary**
> Tarvainen explores creativity and innovation in microenterprises in the welfare services sector in Finland, including medical and dental practices, physiotherapy services, residential care facilities, and home help providers.
>
> Some points for discussion, learning and reflection arising from this paper include:
> - How small enterprises can develop an internal culture of creativity and innovation.
> - The role of the owner-manager in fostering a culture of creativity and innovation.
> - How small enterprises can formulate a creativity and innovation strategy.
> - The challenges and potential of harnessing the creativity of employees in a small enterprise.

Abstract: Entrepreneurship emerges from innovation and continuous creativity enables enterprises to operate, grow and succeed. These concepts, innovation and creativity, are the main ideas of entrepreneurship. The significance of welfare service enterprises especially has fundamentally increased in the 21st century. These enterprises are usually micro-sized and entrepreneurs are deeply committed to their enterprises. Moreover, this business sector is fairly new and there are numerous innovative enterprises. Hence, it is important to analyze the creativity of these especially innovative organizations. This paper introduces the elements of creativity and innovation in the welfare service sector. The strategy of this research is a multiple case study. Nevertheless, this is not a classical case study. In addition, the findings of this research are based on several enterprises and the phenomenon is in focus rather than the cases themselves. More profoundly, the research strategy is also extensive and mixed methods were used. The data were collected from questionnaires, the informants being welfare service entrepreneurs in eastern and north-eastern Finland. Data were analyzed using quantitative and qualitative methods. In summary, the welfare service entrepreneurs valued innovation and creativity. In addition, the enterprises also have an innovation and creativity oriented culture, accordingly they motivate their personnel to operate independently and creatively. Most importantly, the entrepreneurs experienced the innovation aspects as strategic for the operation of their enterprises. In conclusion, the results showed that the ability to innovate and create is regarded as an important success factor in the welfare enterprises. However, the competition in the welfare service sector has intensified. Above all, national medium-sized and larger organizations are taking over the markets and the entrepreneurs also mentioned these actors as a significant threat. The factors which enable welfare microenterprises to continue operating need to be studied. Furthermore, the results showed that the enterprises valued innovation and creativity, and these elements were seen as crucial to their continuation. Nevertheless, creating innovation is not systematic but rather haphazard, even if these enterprises have an innovation-oriented culture. Whether these micro-sized enterprises could be more innovative and creative than national larger organizations, if these activities were more carefully considered is an interesting question.

Keywords: creativity, innovation, welfare service enterprises

1 Introduction

The ability to think creatively is more important than ever before in business and in people's lives (Hong and Milgram 2010), and especially in frequently changing environments (Carmeli, Reiter-Palmon and Ziv 2010). In addition, innovative ability has been seen as an essential element for an organization's operations (Pathak 2008; Hughes 2003), and further, innovations require creativity (Klijn and Tomic 2010, Heunks 1998). Creativity creates innovations, which in turn contribute, for example, to economic, social or ethical values (Hughes 2003). Previous studies have drawn attention to factors which influence creativity and also innovativeness. However, creativity in the field of micro-sized enterprises has not been a major focus in previous studies.

Despite the importance of creativity as a major part of organizational development and entrepreneurship as a remarkable employer, the research of entrepreneurial creativity remains limited. Unfortunately, only few studies have focused on the influence of creativity on enterprises' activities and most of these have concentrated on analyzing the processes of creativity actions, not the effects themselves. This paper scrutinizes aspects of creativity and innovation and how the attitudes of entrepreneurs towards these appear in the welfare service sector. The aim of this study is to define the attitudes of entrepreneurs towards creativity and innovativeness in the field of private welfare services. The welfare service sector especially has been viable in the 21th century in Finland (e.g. Lith 2006) and this development has required creative and innovative activities and individuals. Future studies should examine the relationship between these attitudes and the performance of the enterprises. The implications of this research for future studies and management practices are to discuss the importance of management considerations of creativity for the development of an enterprise. Creativity should be understood as a part of operational and strategic management for increasing and developing performance. This paper aims to pay attention to this phenomenon. Furthermore, this research could guide the practices of further studies. In the following sections, first, the theoretical framework is evaluated, and then the method and empirical background are introduced. Finally, the conclusion, limitations and recommendations for further studies are presented.

2 Theoretical background

An organization is also more adaptable to changes if there is an innovative atmosphere (Geroski and Machin 1992). An organizational culture which supports creative activities is not an obvious but rather a conscious choice by a leader (Carmeli et al. 2010; Amabile 1998). Further, human resource management should also be strategic and support the creativity of personnel (Mumford 2000). Moreover, creative thinking is person-based and divergent thinkers have many solutions to problems, whereas constrictedly thinking persons can create only one solution (Hong and Milgram 2010). Carmeli et al. (2010) observed that being a creative employee requires psychological safety, which frequently depends on inclusive leadership. Consequently, a creative organizational culture requires both support from a leader and creatively thinking individuals. Besides, thinking creatively also demands support from groups inside the organization (Mumford, Dansereau and Yammarino 2000). Moreover, the abilities to think creatively and handle failures should also be noticed and encouraged in the educational sector (Hughes 2003).

An entrepreneur's perceptions and background (e.g. education) contribute especially to the creativity of small firms (Heunks 1998). However, academic intelligence is not a requirement to be a creative individual (e.g. Klijn and

Tomic 2010). The meaning of enterprises to the entrepreneurs is frequently more than a means of earning a living. Entrepreneurs value other indicators of success more highly, for example, customer satisfaction and social responsibility, than financial factors (Ahmad and Seet 2009). Furthermore, the atmosphere in the enterprise can support or discourage innovativeness (Naranjo-Valencia, Jiménez-Jiménez and Sanz-Valle 2011). A creative atmosphere requires for example "freedom, positive challenge, supervisory encouragement, work group supports, organizational encouragement, and sufficient resources" (Amabile 1997; e.g. Carmeli et al. 2010). Furthermore, market environment has an influence on creativity (Katila and Shane 2005). Contextual issues also contribute to ethical decision-making, which correlate positively with creativity (Mumford, Waples, Antes, Brown, Connelly, Murphy, and Devenport 2010).

In Heunks' (1998) opinion the meaning of creativity is to foster innovations and, further, productivity is not significant in younger enterprises. It should also be noted that productivity is not always the purpose of creativity. On the contrary, the purpose could be the further development of operations or services aiming to operate more efficiently and be customer-oriented (Amabile 1997; Heunks 1998; McAdam, Reid, Harris and Mitchell 2008). Measuring innovativeness is complex and indicators or instruments to analyze innovativeness may vary depending on the size of the enterprise or organization. The innovativeness indicators of larger organizations are not entirely suitable in the field of SMEs (Carayannis and Provance 2008). Moreover, classification into innovative and non-innovative firms is not relevant in the meaning of the relations of productivity and growth to innovative actions. In fact, Freel (2000) suggested a classification of three levels; (1) successful innovative actions, (2) failed innovative actions, and (3) non-innovative actions. Naturally, failed innovative actions could impair the performance of an enterprise at several levels in contrast to non-innovative enterprises. The ability for creative thinking and innovative actions is especially valued in times of depression or highly competitive markets (Geroski and Machin 1992).

In Amabile's (1998) model creativity requires three elements: expertise, creative thinking skills and motivation. However, expertise and motivation, for example, do not support creativity in every situation. The expert may have been limited to some special field and be unable to create new things outside this field. The creativity may be domain-specific (Baer 1998) or domain-general or both (Hong and Milgram 2010). Accordingly, both approaches could be suitable depending on the requirements of the business line. Motivation by rewards does not support creativity in every case, in fact, it could decrease creative actions (Amabile 1998), and undermine the trust and cooperation of personnel (Ferrin and Dirks 2003). Thus the intrinsic motivation is the key element to create and be creative (Amabile 1997; Ruscio, Whitney and Amabile 1998). Intrinsic motivation also depends on an individual's age; younger people have been claimed to be more motivated than older ones (Klijn and Tomic 2010). Moreover, people can be motivated by various levels of autonomy or social needs (e.g. support from others) and leaders should recognize both these approaches to achieve an effective motivational strategy (Mumford et al. 2000; Dew 2009).

3 Method

The method of this research is partly a case study, whose objective is to enhance the understanding of how creativity contributes to the vitality of enterprises. But this is not a classical case study, because one of the aims is also to find a new explanation for the vitality of enterprises. Furthermore, the findings of this examination are based on numerous organizations not only a few, which makes this a multiple case study (e.g. Eriksson and Kovalainen 2008). A multiple case study creates understanding from a larger group of objects. In addition, this research is based more on content than theory, since the phenomenon of organizational vitality is not well known. This research concentrated on addressing creative activities as a part of vitality. However, only few articles on the vitality of organizations have been published. Nonetheless these articles have not analyzed vitality themes in the context of welfare services or micro-sized enterprises. The theoretical background of this investigation is the theory of entrepreneurship and creativity and evidence of organizational vitality in a wider perspective. The theories of organizational success, growth and competitiveness are also a part of the background.

The phenomenon is in the focus of this research, not the cases proper. More profoundly, the research strategy of this study is extensive and the aim is to create new understanding and explain the elements which create, promote or destroy vitality in the context of creativeness. Such an approach is not mainly interested in individual cases. Several cases were chosen due the theoretical ambition? to promote as general findings as possible, and to avoid the bias in the data (e.g. Burton-Jones 2009). Every separate case increases the understanding of the phenomenon as a whole. The cases are only instruments which create the larger understanding (e.g. Eriksson and Kovalainen 2008).

Mixed methods were also used (e.g. Miller and Gatta 2006). This study includes both quantitative and qualitative data (e.g. Molina-Azorín 2009). A questionnaire survey was carried out on December 2010. The questionnaires were addressed to all welfare service enterprises of the focal area of this research. The total population of interest was 448 enterprises (Joensuu Regional Development Company 2010; The Federation of Finnish Enterprises 2010). The questions in the questionnaire addressed vitality themes from the literature. Both questions and statements were used and respondents chose the most suitable option from a five-point Likert scale, where 5 meant "totally agree" and 1 "totally disagree". There were also some open-ended questions.

4 Sample

The population of interest was welfare service enterprises in eastern and north-eastern Finland. According to Statistics Finland (2008) welfare service enterprises are divided into three categories. The first section "human health activities" includes services such as "private hospital services, medical and dental practices, and other human health activities such as physical therapy services". The second section "residential care activities" includes services with accommodation for special groups such as "mentally retarded, elderly, disabled persons, and professional family care activities for children and young people". The third section "social work activities without accommodation" includes activities such as "home help services for different special groups and, for example, day-care for children". These categories of Statistics Finland (2008) are not suitable for the purposes of this study, because they are fairly extensive and conceptual. In this study the welfare enterprises are divided into eight business lines based on the answers to the questionnaire. These sections are physiotherapy, residential care, psychotherapy, medical and dental practices, social work activities without accommodation, home help services, other social services such as acupuncture services, and other fields of activity.

The sample consisted of 448 enterprises. Of the questionnaires, 131 were completed and returned, resulting in a 29 percent response rate. Seventy-five percent of responding enterprises were located in eastern Finland

(North Karelia) and 25 percent in north-eastern Finland (Kainuu). Analysis of the enterprises' background information indicated that 59 percent of owners were female, 19 percent were male and 22 percent of enterprises had both female and male owners. Typically they were single entrepreneurs (67 percent). Family enterprises accounted for 38 percent of respondents. The enterprises were primarily 5-10 years old (28 percent), 1-4 years old (25 percent) or 11-20 years old (24 percent). The three main lines of business were residential care (28 percent), physiotherapy (18 percent) and private medical services (12 percent). The enterprises were primarily micro-sized and employed 1-4 employees (76 percent) and 91 percent of enterprises employed 1-20 persons. The mean number of personnel was 2.6 persons and 57 percent of enterprises had only an entrepreneur an no other personnel. The enterprises of interest were located in sparsely populated areas (42 percent) or in cities (38 percent), twenty percent of enterprises were located near cities or in core rural areas.

5 Results

5.1 Analysis of the questionnaire

In the questionnaire the entrepreneurs responded to four statements on innovativeness. They chose suitable response options where 5 = "totally agree" and 1 = "totally disagree". These four statements are as follows: (1) "Our enterprise is innovative", (2) "Our enterprise is more innovative than other similar enterprises", (3) "Innovativeness is essential for the existence of our enterprise", and (4) "Our enterprise supports personnel's creative actions". In the following table (Table 1) values are also categorized based on the age of the enterprises.

According to the questionnaire responses the entrepreneurs considered their enterprises to be innovative. Enterprises less than one year old were reportedly especially innovative, whereas those over 20 years old were the least innovative of all. The welfare service sector as a whole was reportedly quite innovative. Nevertheless, entrepreneurs considered their enterprises quite more innovative than other similar enterprises. Again, the highest mean (3.83) and similarly the lowest standard deviation (.753) were in the group of start-up enterprises, while the lowest mean (3.28) was among enterprises 5-10 years old. Innovativeness was considered a vital element for the survival of an enterprise. Innovativeness as a vital element was essential both to younger and older enterprises, but enterprises less than five years old valued innovativeness rather more than enterprises with established operations. Welfare enterprises supported personnel's creative activities. Similarly innovativeness was been seen as a vital element, the creativity of personnel was deemed essential. Enterprises over 20 years old valued creative activities among personnel less (mean 4.05) than did newer enterprises (means 4.35-4.67), nonetheless the mean value of the oldest group is still significantly high.

Table 1: Enterprises' innovative activities on various age levels

	Below one year		1-4 years		5-10 years		11-20 years		Over 20 years	
	Mean	SD	Mean	SD	Mean	SD	Mean	SD	Mean	SD
Our enterprise is innovative	4.17	.753	4.00	.871	3.97	1.075	4.07	.730	3.76	.995
Our enterprise is more innovative than others	3.83	.753	3.36	1.062	3.28	1.023	3.70	.993	3.38	1.024
Innovativeness is essential for the existence of our enterprise	4.00	.707	4.07	.980	3.81	1.120	4.08	1.017	3.81	.873
Our enterprise supports personnel's creative actions	4.40	.548	4.38	.970	4.35	.977	4.67	.620	4.05	.740

Table 2 presents the summary of statistics. Note that among these four statements the Cronbach's Alpha is 0.797.

Table 2: Summary item statistics

	Mean	Minimum	Maximum	Range	Variance	N of Items	Cronbach's Alpha
Item Means	3.95	3.45	4.38	.923	.143	4	.797

The correlations are introduced in Table 3. The enterprises considered themselves innovative, and also more innovative than other similar enterprises. Moreover, innovativeness was a vital element. The personnel's creative activities were deemed significant, but this statement correlates with the statement "Our enterprise is innovative" more than with other statements. The entrepreneurs supported less personnel's creativity for achieving greater creativeness and the personnel's creativeness was less important for the survival of enterprise even if the mean values of these statements were also high (Table 1).

Table 3: Correlations

		Our enterprise is innovative	Our enterprise supports personnel's creative actions	Our enterprise is more innovative than others
Our enterprise supports personnel's creative actions	Pearson Correlation	.564**		
	Covariance	.417		
	N	105		
Our enterprise is more innovative than others	Pearson Correlation	.627**	.362**	
	Covariance	.582	.301	
	N	116	105	
Innovativeness is essential for the existence of our enterprise	Pearson Correlation	.634**	.294**	.605**
	Covariance	.577	.238	.613
	N	117	104	114

**. Correlation is significant at the 0.01 level (2-tailed).

In conclusion, innovativeness was essential to welfare enterprises of various ages. The mean values of two age categories; below one year, and 11-20 years, were higher in every statement than the total mean of all enterprises, whereas 5-10-year and over 20-year-old enterprises were under the total means in every statement. Moreover, the correlations between the statements of enterprise's innovativeness and compared to other enterprises, and the importance of innovativeness were notable.

5.2 Analysis of open-ended responses

The open section included two questions, (1) "Which three elements are important to the vitality of your enterprise?", (2) "Which three elements are important to the competitiveness of your enterprise?".

The analysis of the open-ended responses highlighted interesting questions. Innovativeness was not a common answer to the question of organizational vitality or competitiveness, even if it was mentioned as crucial to the operation of the enterprise in the questionnaire section. Firstly, a total of 100 entrepreneurs answered the question on organizational vitality. Eight entrepreneurs mentioned innovation or creativity as a vitality element. Respondents were mainly from the field of residential care (three enterprises) and located in sparsely populated areas (four enterprises). Mainly (four enterprises) these were start-up enterprises (under four years old) or at the age of 5-10 years old (three enterprises). Secondly, in the question on organizational competitive elements there were a total 102 answers. Innovativeness or creativity were mentioned by seven entrepreneurs. Mainly (four enterprises) these entrepreneurs were in the field of other welfare services (e.g. acupuncture, family counseling or therapy, and other social therapy services). The enterprises (five enterprises) were located in sparsely populated areas and were mainly at the stage of start-up (three enterprises) or aged of 5-10 years (two enterprises).

In conclusion, the innovativeness and creativity seemed to be an important vitality element especially to residential care services, whereas the elements of competitiveness were reportedly more important in other welfare services. The enterprises in sparsely populated areas and those aged under ten years valued innovativeness and creativity as a vitality or competitive element. However, the results of the open-ended responses are not extensive due the lack of respondents. Either way, innovativeness and creativity were noted as a part of enterprise's existence.

5.3 Enterprise's strategic activity

Welfare service enterprises are usually micro- and small-sized and the entrepreneur is both a manager and a part of the personnel. Therefore the meaning of strategy could be complex. Several enterprises had no written strategy, but nonetheless the entrepreneur had planned and committed to a strategy. Probably for this reason, the discrepancy in the responses about written strategy was remarkably high (total 1.440; Table 4), whereas in the answers about innovativeness the deviation was less (highest value 1.011). The start-up enterprises had a business plan and a strategy, while from one to ten years after establishment the strategy required updating. Again, enterprises aged 11-20 years more frequently had a written strategy. However, this study was not able to analyze innovativeness as a strategic action. In spite of this, the answers show similarities between activity of innovation or strategic actions between the various age levels. The enterprises should also consider the importance of strategy to operational management, and further creativity and innovativeness as a part of strategic management.

Table 4: Existence of written strategy

Our enterprise has a written strategy		
Age of the enterprise	Mean	Std. Deviation
Below one year	4.17	.983
1-4 years	3.58	1.523
5-10 years	3.19	1.575
11-20 years	4.45	1.121
Over 20 years	3.50	1.235
Total	3.70	1.440

6 Discussion

This study considered innovativeness among welfare enterprises in eastern and north-eastern Finland. The results indicate that these enterprises consider themselves innovative. Furthermore, innovativeness is of the utmost importance to them, as Pett and Wolff (2009) also found in their research. Enterprises also valued personnel and its active creative thinking. Even if the enterprises seemed innovative and creative, they diverged in activity at various age levels. Sager and Dowling (2009) likewise found in their research that strategic activities in the field of marketing could depend on a company's life cycle stage. In this study enterprises aged below one year and between 11 and 20 years were more active in every statement than other enterprises.

The results of the questionnaire showed that the enterprises appreciated innovativeness and creative thinking. However, the open-ended responses about vitality and competitive elements did not support these results. According to this study the enterprises were innovative, but innovativeness as the element of vitality or competitiveness only concerned a few enterprises. In addition, a strategic entrepreneurship approach promotes creativity and innovation, especially among employees and the approach was deemed necessary (e.g. Harms, Schulz, Kraus, and Fink 2009). Innovativeness was based significantly on leadership, organizational culture, continuous improvement, knowledge management and demands of markets (McAdam et al. 2008). Accordingly, the analysis of an enterprise's strategic innovativeness requires deep and wide analysis, and consideration of all these factors (e.g. Woodman, Sawyer and Griffin 1993).

This study has limitations in that it concerns one industry in two areas of Finland and the population of interest was not substantial. Moreover, the data collected were not comprehensive. However, these results are interesting and the phenomenon requires more studies with larger samples in several areas and with larger data collections of both quantitative and qualitative material. Nonetheless, the aim of this paper was not to generalize (e.g. Onwuegbuzie and Leech 2010), but to introduce the aspects of innovativeness in the field of welfare services. The results could advise both entrepreneurs and researchers to consider the innovativeness and creative atmosphere as strategic decisions. These aspects were important according the results, but this study was not able to ascertain how these aspects affected the daily or strategic operations and performance. Innovativeness seemed essential and could also be a competitive advantage, especially in highly competitive markets (e.g. Geroski and Machin 1992).

The importance of innovativeness and creativity to younger enterprises should be studied, likewise which factors explain the difficulties in middle-aged enterprises. Another interesting question is, does a location in a sparsely populated area contribute to innovativeness? In this study the location of enterprises was only addressed in the open-ended responses, whereas the age of an enterprise was of interest in the questionnaire. Moreover, future studies should address if innovativeness is important at all to vitality or competitiveness. Consequently, it would be interesting to analyze whether an enterprise reportedly valuing innovativeness as a vitality or competitive element differs those enterprises not valuing innovativeness or creativity. Furthermore, this study did not estimate innovativeness as a strategic activity among enterprises, but this raised the discussion of the correlation of these elements. Drejer (2008) proposed that innovativeness should be managed and also perceived as a part of strategic decision-making, but managing creativity is no simple operation (Huber 1998). Hence, future work should examine more specifically if enterprises' strategies include innovative activities or if innovativeness in general was a strategic element. The need to improve strategic creativity should be noted. In fact, systematic creativity management can make a real contribution to an enterprise's performance.

References

Ahmad, N.H. and Seet, P-S. (2009) "Understanding Business Success through the Lens of SME Founder-Owners in Australia and Malaysia", *International Journal of Entrepreneurial Venturing*, Vol 1, No. 1, pp 72-87.

Amabile, T.M. (1997) "Motivating Creativity in Organizations: on Doing what You Love and Loving what You Do", *California Management Review*, vol 40, No. 1 (Fall), pp 39-58.

Amabile, T.M. (1998) "How to Kill Creativity", *Harvard Business Review*, September-October, pp 77-87.

Baer, J. (1998) "The Case for Domain Specificity of Creativity", *Creativity Research Journal*, Vol 11, No. 2, pp 173-177.

Burton-Jones, A. (2009) "Minimizing Method Bias Through Programmatic Research", *MIS Quarterly*, Vol 33, No. 3, September, pp 445-471.

Carayannis, E.G. and Provance, M. (2008) "Measuring Firm Innovativeness: towards a Composite Innovation Index Built on Firm Innovative Posture, Propensity and Performance Attributes", *International Journal of Innovation and Regional Development*, Vol 1, No. 1, pp 90-107.

Carmeli, A., Reiter-Palmon, R. and Ziv, E. (2010) "Inclusive Leadership and Employee Involvement in Creative Tasks in the Workplace: The Mediating Role of Psychological Safety", *Creativity Research Journal*, Vol 22, No. 3, pp 250-260.

Dew, R. (2009) "Creative Resolve Response: How Changes in Creative Motivation Relate to Cognitive Style", *Journal of Management Development*, Vol 28, No. 10, pp 945-966.

Drejer, A. (2008) "Are You Innovative Enough?", *International Journal of Innovation and Learning*, Vol 5, No. 1, pp 1-17.

Eriksson, P. and Kovalainen, A. (2008) *Qualitative Methods in Business Research*, Sage Publications Ltd. United Kingdom.

Ferrin, D.L. and Dirks, K.T. (2003) "The Use of Rewards to Increase and Decrease Trust: Mediating Processes and Differential Effects", *Organization Science*, Vol 14, No. 1, January-February, pp 18-31.

Freel, M.S. (2000) "Do Small Innovating Firms Outperform Non-Innovators?", *Small Business Economics*, Vol 14, pp 195-210.

Geroski, P. and Machin, S. (1992) "Do innovating Firms Outperform Non-Innovators?", *Business Strategy Review*, Summer, pp 79-90.

Harms, R., Schulz, A., Kraus, S. and Fink, M. (2009) "The Conceptualisation of 'Opportunity' in Strategic Management Research", *International Journal of Entrepreneurial Venturing*, Vol 1, No. 1, pp 57-71.

Heunks, F.J. (1998) "Innovation, Creativity and Success", *Small Business Economics*, Vol 10, pp 263-272.

Hong, E. and Milgram, R.M. (2010) "Creative Thinking Ability: Domain Generality and Specificity", *Creativity Research Journal*, Vol 22, No. 3, pp 272-228.
Huber, J.C. (1998) "Invention and Inventivity is a Random, Poisson Process: A Potential Guide to Analysis of General Creativity", *Creativity Research Journal*, Vol 11, No. 3, pp 231-241.
Hughes, G.D. (2003) "Add Creativity to Your Decision Processes", *The Journal for Quality & Participation*, Vol 26, No. 2, pp 4-13.
Joensuu Regional Development Company, JOSEK Ltd. (2010) "The company register of North Karelia", [online], http://yritysrekisteri.josek.fi/PublicSearchResults.aspx.
Katila, R. and Shane, S. (2005) "When Does Lack of Resources Make New Firms Innovative?", *Academy of Management Journal*, Vol 48, No. 5, pp 814-829.
Klijn, M. and Tomic, W. (2010) "A Review of Creativity within Organizations from a Psychological Perspective", *Journal of Management Development*, Vol 29, No. 4, pp 322-343.
Lith, P. (2006) *Yritystoiminta ja kuntien ostopalvelut sosiaali- ja terveydenhuollossa*, KTM Julkaisuja 25/2006, Kauppa- ja teolllisuusministeriö, Helsinki.
McAdam, R., Reid, R., Harris, R. and Mitchell, N. (2008) "Key Determinants of Organisational and Technological Innovation in UK SMEs: an Empirical Study", *International Journal of Entrepreneurship and Innovation Management*, Vol 8, No. 1, pp 1-14.
Miller, S.I. and Gatta, J.L. (2006) " The Use of Mixed Methods Models and Designs in the Human Sciences: Problems and Prospects", *Quality & Quantity*, Vol 40, pp 595-610.
Molina-Azorín, J.F. (2009) "Understanding How Mixed Methods Research Is Undertaken within a Specific Research Community: The Case of Business Studies", *International Journal of Multiple Research Approaches*, Vol 3, No. 1 (April), pp 47-57.
Mumford, M.D. (2000) "Managing Creative People: Strategies and Tactics for Innovation", *Human Resource Management Review*, Vol 10, No. 3, pp 313-351.
Mumford, M.D., Dansereau, F. and Yammarino, F.J. (2000) "Followers, Motivations, and Level of Analysis: The Case of Individualized Leadership", *Leadership Quarterly*, Vol 11, No. 3, pp 313-340.
Mumford, M.D., Waples, E.P., Antes, A.L., Brown, R.P., Connelly, S., Murphy, S.T. and Devenport, L.D. (2010) "Creativity and Ethics: The Relationship of Creative and Ethical Problem-Solving", *Creativity Research Journal*, Vol 22, No. 1, pp 74-78.
Naranjo-Valencia, J.C., Jiménez-Jiménez, D. and Sanz-Valle, R. (2011) "Innovation or Imitation? The Role of Organizational Culture", *Management Decision*, Vol 49, No. 1, pp 55-72.
Onwuegbuzie, A.J. and Leech, N.L. (2010) "Generalization Practices in Qualitative Research: a Mixed Methods Case Study", *Quality & Quantity*, Vol 44, pp 881-892.
Pathak, R.D. (2008) "Grass-root Creativity, Innovation, Entrepreneurialism and Poverty Reduction", *International Journal of Entrepreneurship and Innovation Management*, Vol 8, No. 1, pp 87-98.
Pett, T.L. and Wolff, T.A. (2009) "SME Opportunity for Growth or Profit: What is the Role of Product and Process Improvement?", *International Journal of Entrepreneurial Venturing*, Vol 1, No. 1, pp 5-21.
Ruscio, J., Whitney, D.M. and Amabile, T.M. (1998) "Looking Inside the Fishbowl of Creativity: Verbal and Behavioral Predictors of Creative Performance", *Creativity Research Journal*, Vol 11, No. 3, pp 243-263.
Sager, B. and Dowling, M. (2009) "Strategic Marketing Planning for Opportunity Exploitation in Young Entrepreneurial Companies", *International Journal of Entrepreneurial Venturing*, Vol 1, No. 1, pp 88-107.

Leading Issues in Innovation Research

Statistic Finland. (2008) "Standard Industrial Classification 2008", [online], www.stat.fi/meta/luokitukset/toimiala/910-2008/index_en.html.
The Federation of Finnish Enterprises. (2010) "The Company Register of Kainuu", [online], www.yrittajat.fi/fi-Fl/yrityshaku/haku/.
Woodman, R.W., Sawyer, J.E. and Griffin, R.W. (1993) "Toward a Theory of Organizational Creativity", *Academy of Management Review*, Vol 18, No. 2, pp 293-321.

Tiina Tarvainen

Analysis of the Relationship Between the Company's Internal Resources and the Effectiveness of Innovative Activity of SMEs in Poland

Tomasz Norek
Department of Innovation Effectiveness, Faculty of Management and Economics of Services, University of Szczecin, Szczecin, Poland
Originally published in The Proceedings of ICIE 2014

> **Editorial commentary**
> Through a study of SMEs in Poland, Norek considers the relationship between a firm's internal resources and its innovative activity. Norek notes that metrics on innovation in Poland indicate that the country is not as advanced as other economies, and that, in particular, the SME community in Poland lags behind that of some other economies in Europe with regard to innovation activity.
>
> Some points for discussion, learning and reflection arising from this paper include:
> - Innovation strategy formulation in SMEs.
> - How to determine and assess the innovation potential of an SME.
> - Using internal resources to maximise innovation potential in an SME.
> - The role of SMEs in increasing innovation activity in transition economies.

Abstract: The analysis of innovative activity of companies very often indicates that the innovations introduced to the market do not bring the expected benefits. This leads to the conclusion that very often innovation activities of enterprises are inefficient. The modern model for the innovative activity indicates that one of the key factors for success of innovative activity of enterprises is properly implemented the introduction of new solutions to market. The problem of diffusion of innovation involves a number of issues related to the process of spreading and promoting innovation in the market. It is widely recognized that the powers of innovation diffusion is an important determinant of the capacity of firms. This article is an attempt to examine relationship between the company's internal resources and the effectiveness of innovative activity. To achieve this research objective author formulated the hypothesis: There is the relationship between the company's internal resources and the effectiveness of innovative activity. This paper will present the results of empirical research conducted by the author among Polish SMEs in the years 2009 – 2012.

Keywords: innovations, the effectiveness of innovative processes

1 Introduction

In today's economy it is widely accepted paradigm of innovation. It is recommended to businesses to conduct innovative activities which are by definition should generate profits and increase competitiveness. The paradigm of innovation is confirmed by several studies. On the basis of these studies are also commonly formulated a recognized economic development strategies. Meanwhile, innovative activity is often inefficient and do not deliver the expected results. This problem is particularly noticeable in the case of SMEs.

Poland is presently in specific moment of its development. Previous competitive advantages based on law work costs are more and more vividly losing their significance. It becomes necessary to create new advantages based on knowledge and innovation forming a main factor of the long-term economic growth. From this point of view, it is crucial to develop innovative activities of companies, including research and development, as the most important factors of the competitiveness in global scale.

Unfortunately, the innovation of Polish economy is relatively low. In Innovation Union Scoreboard report, published in 2011 by InnoMetrics research institute, commissioned by the European Commission, the Polish economy in view of innovation expressed with SII (*Summary Innovation Index*) has been located at the 23rd position with 27 EU member countries researched (the value of the aggregate SII ration for Poland = 0, 296, the value of the averaged ration for EU27=0,539) [1].

The low innovation of the Polish economy is especially noticeable for the small and medium businesses sector, which may have negative conse-

---

[1] http://www.proinno-europe.eu/page/summary-innovation-index-0#_ftn2

quences related, among others, to the decrease of the competitiveness of the economy and its marginalisation on the international arena. This aspect is frequently addressed in numerous scientific publications and reports considering the condition of the Polish economy's innovation – among others, the publications by: E. Horodyńska-Okoń, W. Świtalski, M. Zastępowski.

Simultaneously, many national researches (and some statistics published e.g. by GUS [Central Statistical Office]) reveal that Polish companies frequently declare a relatively high level of own innovation – especially in the aspect of introducing to the market innovative goods and services or the absorption of innovative solutions - A. Żołnierski PARP Report [Innovation of Polish Companies 2011].

The revealed cognitive dichotomy indicates the existence of possible differences in methodological defining and understanding the innovation or omitting during the evaluation of the innovative activities, the aspects related to results that should be caused by such activities – despite the fact that the researched companies more and more frequently declare implementation of the innovative undertakings, the efficiency of such actions is not reflected in the companies' results.

2 Company innovation potential: Review of the literature

The innovation of a given country's economy is mainly determined by the innovation of companies that operate in the economy. The innovation of the companies is influenced by internal factors (including, above all, potential and resources of a company, plus intellectual capital, material, financial and organizational resources). Additionally, the development of enterprise innovation abilities is influenced by the particulars of the industry and sector, where the company operates and external factors (including national conditions [e.g., legal regulations related to innovation support activities] and region-specific conditions [e.g., legal, culture, economic and technical factors).

Analysis of all of the modern models of enterprise innovation (Norek 2012; Tidd and Bessant 2011) and research on the scope of innovation determinants (Lager, 2011) reveals that the key factor that regulates efficiency in the innovation processes is internal the enterprises' innovation potential.

Tomasz Norek

The theory of innovation potential is based on the concept of company resources. This concept, developed at the beginning of the 1990s, assumes that a company's ability to develop all of the aspects of activity is closely related to the possessed resources. Edith Penrose (1959) was an early proponent of this outlook. Her publications have revealed the role of resources in the formation of company competitive advantage and the increase theory (Hall and Rosenberg, 2010).

A detailed analysis of the factors that determine company innovation potential is subject to numerous studies and scientific publications. It seems that the most global view of the factors that determine company innovation potential was suggested by Birchall and Armstrong (2001), who created a model of innovation conditions that includes the following factors: external environment, internal environment, innovation process and development management.

Tidd et al. (2001) held a somewhat different view of innovation determinants and focused in particular on internal organizational factors that stimulate the innovation processes. The most important include, among others: visionary leadership, appropriate organizational structure, recruitment, the willingness to engage in the innovation process, ability to conduct teamwork or the readiness to learn and adopt new solutions.

In the Polish literature, the analysis has been presented, among others, in works by Białoń (2010), Poznańska (1998) and Żołnierski (2005). The most precise seems to be the interpretation suggested by Żołnierski (2005), who suggested that a company's innovation potential is determined by the internal innovation potential as well as the access to external sources of information necessary for the innovation process.

In sum, innovation ability or potential determine a company's ability to create innovations. By analogy, it may be stated that the lack of innovation potential is a barrier to the companies' effective innovation processes.

In addition to the definition of the essence and the role of innovation potential in the innovation process, an issue is the measurement of individual determinants of innovation potential. A considerable part of factors that significantly affect the innovative capacity of a company (particularly as related to external factors) are difficult to measure or to quantify, which, to a large extent, makes it difficult to analyze and evaluate these issues precisely (Fagerberg, 2004).

A company, in practice, can influence only internal factors in the process of conscious formation of innovative capacity and the creation of a strategy related to innovative activity for the long term. For this reason, ability to analyze and evaluate internal factors that constitute enterprise innovative capacity become extremely important. Recently, discussions about the determinants that affect enterprise innovativeness and methods of innovativeness measurement have gained significant meaning. This discussion, supported by numerous publications, has both the academic and practical dimension, as it is economic practice that is remarkably interested in effective tools for the measurement and evaluation of innovative capacity and the effectiveness of innovative processes that occur in companies (Cook 2011; Prahalad and Krishnam 2011).

The indicated multisidedness and complexity of the phenomena that form the innovative capacity of enterprises forces one to search for optimum methods by which to analyze and evaluate this area. This problem particularly applies to SME sector enterprises. Various publications have suggested new methods for the measurement of innovative capacity and potential of the enterprises that precisely account for the special character of operations performed and the effect of the regional conditions on the innovativeness of the enterprise. New proposals for the measurement of innovative potential very often assume different measurement methods for different sizes of companies or groups of companies (e.g., service companies; (Kaplan and Norton 2009; Kanerva et al., 2006) or high-tech companies (Miles 2004). The authors of these proposals have indicated that in the implementation of the innovative process in companies belonging to various industries or sectors, there are such great differences that the use of one method of innovative potential measurement very often leads to incorrect results. Such a situation forces one to conduct in-depth studies designed to capture the actual innovative potential of companies.

3 The essence of effectiveness of innovative activity implemented by companies

The analysis of the literature on the subject indicates that the issue of the efficiency of innovative actions is relatively seldom addressed (among others: Arundell, Bloch, Rosebusch, Sawang), and the Polish literature practically does not present a full elaboration considering the influence of company's resources on the efficiency of innovative actions (among others: Karaganov, Karasek, Wach, Zastępowski).

The efficiency is measured (both ex post and ex ante) with the use of index methods, based on the partial synthetical productivity indicators of the resource usage (e.g. work, capital). The calculation of ex ante efficiency estimates the anticipated effects with the use of specific means or time. The ex post efficiency is implied to determine the results of the specific tasks' implementation.

The authors undertaking the subject of evaluating the innovative activity's efficiency try above all to define the efficiency of the innovative activity (usually in relation to defining the efficiency of other types of company activities) and apply classic efficiency measures, usually based on the measurable features of innovative activity.

As indicated in the literature (e.g. Brzeziński, 2001, p.146) the innovative activity is basically evaluated with the same methods as used for the evaluation of investment projects. Thus, the wide scope of innovation forms is brought to technological, production or process shape, as those the effects of which may be evaluated with financial measures. However a problem occurs e.g. in case of the value innovation or even the organizational innovation, when it is hard to specify an expected rate of return and the prospected market success – due to the complexity and multidimensionality of possible effects and costs. Thus there are suggestions to distinguish the evaluation of the efficiency of purely capital investments and the evaluation of the innovation usage, since these undertakings have different goals and methods of their implementation, results, methodology of specifying expenditures and results, conditions of evaluating the results and the influence on changes of other activity indicators (Karganov, 2008, p.135-136).

The above observations prove the necessity to undertake detailed researches in relation to the nature of innovative processes' efficiency and determine an attempt to elaborate methods of measuring the efficiency of innovative activities that in the fullest way would take into consideration the nature and complexity of the innovative processes.

The starting point for creating the methodology for the evaluation of innovative activity's efficiency may be a detailed analysis of innovative processes that take place in companies.

4 The measurement of innovative activity on the basis of the analysis of innovation diffusion

The implementation of innovative projects – regardless of the size of company which implements the innovation and regardless of the type of the implemented innovation - takes place according to the diagram which is defined in the subject literature as the model of the innovative process (Drucker 1994, p.35). Actually the best known examples of subsequent descriptions of the implementation of an innovative process include: the *"chain-linked model of the innovative process"* suggested by S.J. Kline and N. Rosenberg (Kline, Rosenberg 1986, p 289-290) and the *"integrated model"* described by R. Rothwell and W. Zegveld (Rothwell, Zegveld, 1985).

Further research on the essence of the implementation of innovative projects, the development of the innovation theory and the practice concerning innovative activities led to the creation of subsequent evolution models of innovative processes. The authors of the new proposals integrated the implementation of the innovative process with virtually each area of a company's activity, showing that the resources owned by the company determine its innovative potential – namely the ability to effectively and efficiently implement innovative projects (Norek 2012). The currently binding models of the implementation of innovative projects include the model of: "the 5th generation innovative process" (Rothwell 1995), the spiral innovation process (Oslo Manual 2005), the efficient management of innovation (Tidda, Bessant, Pavitt 2001).

Analyzing the contemporary models, it may be clearly stated that the Authors of each of the new proposals emphasize the significance of the stage related to diffusion and popularization of the implemented innovation.

The diffusion of innovation, defined by the Oslo manual, means the "dissemination of innovation by market and non-market channels, starting from the first implementation at any place in the world" and "the way in which innovations are subject to dissemination by market and non-market channels, from the first implementation to the contact with various consumers" (Oslo Manual 2005, p. 80).

To sum up the above discussions, it may be concluded that the diffusion of innovation determines the principles of market commercialization of innovative products and services and is an element of the innovative process which is directly responsible for the market success of new products and services. Therefore, it may be concluded that innovations would not have an economic significance without diffusion processes (Klincewicz 2011, p.22), which makes many researchers acknowledge the issues of diffusion as crucial for a successful implementation of innovative processes (Klein, Sorra 1996, Angle, Van de Ven 2000).

Furthermore, emphasizing the significance of innovation diffusion issues, it should be indicated that knowledge with regard to the diffusion of innovation is necessary to create product and marketing strategies in companies introducing innovative products and services.

Accepting the previously suggested understanding of the efficiency of innovative activity, in the process of efficiency evaluation, both on the ground of diffusion and absorption, a series of indicators may be applied. This may be exemplified with:
- Innovation sale level.
- Success indicator related to the sale of innovation.
- Innovation level of the researched companies.
- Customers' acceptance level in relation to new products and services.
- Efficiency level of diffusion processes for new products and services

In this article the author shall analyse the efficiency of the innovation diffusion processes in Polish SMEs.

5 The analysis of the relationship between the company's internal resources and the effectiveness of innovative activity of SMEs in Poland: Research method

On examining the causes of low innovation of companies from the small and medium businesses sector (Norek 2013) the author has paid special attention to the barriers related to the efficiency of the innovative process implementation. The author has performed a detailed analysis of the relation between the company's innovation level, the sale of innovative products and services, indicator of the achieved success and interrelation between the customers' acceptance of a new product or service and possibility of its market commercialisation.

On the analysis of the above features the author has formed the following research hypothesises: There is the relationship between the company's internal resources and the effectiveness of innovative activity.
The set research goal has been implemented on the basis of logical induction method based on the analysis of processes of innovation diffusion in the companies of small and medium businesses sector. The research includes the evaluation of relationship between the company's internal resources and the effectiveness of innovative activity of SMEs in Poland.

The research has been conducted with the use of the research questionnaire consisting of 43 questions, divided into eight categories – stages of the innovative process implemented in the company.

This research hypothesis has a research aim, which is the analysis and evaluation of internal innovation potential of companies of the small and medium business sector in Poland to identify the barriers that prevent effective implementation of innovation processes. The research goal has been achieved in these studies based on logical induction and analysis of all of the crucial, internal determinants that influence enterprise innovation abilities as well as the classic static analysis.

Preparing a research tool and a range of research, I conduced a detailed review of global research in the field of innovation potential and drew upon the experience of other authors. In particular, I took into account the results of research carried out by Miller (1983) and Zahra and Wicklund

(2010; research on the level of innovation), Koberg et al. (2003; research on communication in organizations), Cameron and Quinn (2003; research on organizational culture). The detailed methodology of the research and the full scope of the study are described in other publications by the author (Norek 2011).

Within the evaluation of individual categories, the companies performed the evaluation of the selected aspects of functioning within a given area. The research was conducted with a use of an Internet questionnaire during the period from April 2010 to August 2012. 200 companies were selected for analysis. They were selected in a purposeful manner to ensure an appropriate research structure: 45% of production companies, 55% of service companies. The division due to the size of the examined companies was as follows: 39% micro enterprises, 47% small enterprises, 13% medium enterprises. The sample for comparative researches was standardized with statistical methods taking into consideration the structure of individual provinces' economy: size of the company and dominant type of the conducted activity. The author is fully aware that the analysed sample is not representative, however it is an amount sufficient to perform the analysis and make conclusions. Structure of the research sample is presented in Table 1.

Table 1: Structure of the research sample

Size of the companies	Type of activity		Total sum
	Production	Service	
Small	41	53	94
Micro	36	43	79
Medium	13	14	27
Total sum	90	110	200

Source: own elaboration

In order to confirm hypotheses author applied the two-step analysis. The first step was the analysis of the innovation potential of the surveyed companies. This analysis allowed the precise determination of the factors affecting the innovation of enterprises. The second step was the analysis of the effectiveness of the innovative activity the surveyed companies. Summary of the study is to analyze the relationship between the company's internal resources and the effectiveness of innovative activity

The Author examined in detail, among others, the following characteristics describing the innovation potential of surveyed companies and process of innovation diffusion:
- Analysis of the internal and external situations of the company,
- Issues concerning the search for ideas with regard to innovation,
- Issues concerning project planning with regard to innovation,
- Financing of innovative projects.,
- Innovation culture and strategy of human resources development,
- Company internal communication and its organization,
- Issues concerning diffusion and transfer of innovation into the market, and
- Level of innovation sales.
- Indicator of success related to innovation sales.
- Level of innovation of examined companies.
- Level of acceptance of customers with regard to new products and services.
- Level of effectiveness of diffusion processes for new products and services.
- Issues concerning implementation of innovative projects.

In Table No. 2 presents the aggregated values for the innovative potential of the enterprises surveyed in the analyzed areas (darker color highlights below average in the distribution).

The analysis of obtained results allows to state that the examined companies demonstrate the lowest internal innovative potential with regard to innovative culture (whole sample is 2.3), evaluating and planning innovative activities (whole sample is 2.2) as well as communication and organization (whole sample is is 2.4). Such low result in these categories may be caused by the lack of experience of examined companies related to innovation, historical lack of innovation culture in Polish SME companies and the continuously lasting transition of Polish economy (from centrally planned to free-market). It should be noted that, in spite of a low innovative potential in most of the researched categories, the analyzed companies evaluated their own capacity with regard to transferring the results of innovative activities onto the market very highly.

Table 2: Aggregate values for the innovation capacity of enterprises surveyed

Type of business/ Stages of the innovation process	Type of operations						Size of the enterprise								
	Production			Services			Micro			Small			Average		
	2010	2011	2012	2010	2011	2012	2010	2011	2012	2010	2011	2012	2010	2011	2012
Culture of innovation and human resources development strategy	2,1	2,2	2,4	1,9	2,1	2,2	1,3	1,5	1,5	2,1	2,3	2,3	2,5	2,9	2,9
Internal communication within the company and its organization	2,4	2,4	2,3	2,6	2,5	2,5	1,8	1,8	1,8	2,2	2,3	2,3	3	3	3
Diffusion of innovation and commercialization	1,9	2,2	3,2	1,8	2,0	3,1	1,4	1,8	2,5	1,6	1,9	3,8	3,6	3,6	3,8
The issue of implementation of innovative	3	3	3,1	2,7	2,7	2,8	2,9	3	3,1	2,9	3	3,3	4	3,4	3,4
Financing of innovative projects	2	2	1,8	2,1	2,2	1,9	2,8	2,8	2,5	3,1	3	2,7	4	3,6	3,5
The issue of planning projects in the field of innovation	1,9	2	2	2	2	2,1	1,8	1,8	1,7	2	2	2,1	3,7	3,5	3,5
Problem of seeking ideas for innovation	3,2	3	3,1	3,1	3	3	2,4	2,5	2,5	3	3,1	3,3	3,5	3,7	3,8
Analysis of the situation and environment	2,1	2,2	2,2	1,9	2	2	2,8	2,7	2,8	3,1	3	4,2	4	4	4
Innovative potential	2,5	2,6	2,6	2,4	2,5	2,6	2,3	2,3	2,3	2,8	2,8	3,0	3,6	3,5	3,5

Source: own elaboration

A positive aspect is the fact that the examined companies, over the three analyzed years, increased the innovative potential in most of the evaluated categories, the general change of innovative potential of the examined companies amounted to 2.44%. The examined companies in the analyzed period (2010-2012) increased the innovative potential the most with regard to innovative culture (change by 14.29% between the first and the third research) and with regard to the analysis of the situation and environment (change by 8.81% between the first and the third research). On the other hand, the biggest decrease in the potential of the examined companies occurred in the category financing (change by -11.21% between the first and the third research) and in the category communication and organization (change by -1.38% between the first and the third research) - which may also be explained by a reduced availability of financial funds for innovative activities.

The level of innovation of a unit is defined as a share of new products or services in its offer in the period of the last three years, regardless whether they were a market success. The notion of "success indicator", on the other hand, should be understood as the share of new products or services in a company's offer in the last five years which, after implementation, gained approval of the market. The evaluation here is supplemented by indicators with regard to the relations of revenue and profit from the sale of new products/services as compared to the company's turnover in the last three years. Those companies for which the values of the abovementioned indicators exceeded the level of 30% should be considered as distinctive in this respect. If, on the other hand, they oscillate within the range of 1%, these entities are in the weakest group of the examined ones. Such a description of ranges is generally adopted in the research concerning the innovativeness of companies or innovation audits. The aggregated results have been presented in Table no. 3.

Table 3: Key indicators describing effectiveness of implementation of innovation diffusion in examined companies

Group	Category	< 1%	2% - 10%	11% - 20%	21%-30%	> 30%
Services	Sale of innovations	27%	27%	22%	18%	6%
	Success indicator	31%	29%	19%	17%	5%
	Level of innovation	29%	24%	23%	19%	5%
Production	Sale of innovations	25%	30%	22%	14%	9%
	Success indicator	15%	23%	27%	25%	10%
	Level of innovation	24%	22%	26%	20%	8%
All	Sale of innovations	26%	28%	22%	16%	8%
	Success indicator	23%	26%	23%	21%	7%
	Level of innovation	27%	23%	25%	19%	6%

Source: own elaboration

The obtained results indicate that half of the examined companies (50%) has a low innovation level (innovation level <10%) which classifies them in the category of non-innovative companies. Only 6% of the examined companies may be considered as innovative, namely such which implemented new products or services in the period of the last three years (innovation level > 10%). These results show that the examined companies do not have a sufficient innovative potential which makes it possible to implement innovative projects. The Author's other research confirms this thesis and indicate that the examined companies demonstrate the lowest innovative potential in the following areas: evaluating and planning innovative activities, communication and organization or financing innovative operations (Norek 2012).

The abovementioned results may be supplemented by an indicator describing the market acceptance of the introduced innovations – namely, in fact, describing the effectiveness of the diffusion process. This indicator is very unfavorable for the examined companies. As much as 49% of the examined companies evaluate the indicator of success below 10%. On the other hand, only 7% percent of the implemented innovations obtained the market's acceptance – indicator of success above 30%. The obtained values should be considered as a clear proof of poor effectiveness of the implementation processes of the implementation of innovation diffusion in the examined companies resulting from an inadequate potential in this aspect. The financial dimension of the weaknesses of the implementation of innovation diffusion processes is characterized by the indicator of innovation sales. As much as 54% of the examined companies declare that profits from the sale of innovations are below 10% of the total profit, and only 8% of the examined companies declare over 30% of profit from the sale of innovations.The obtained results indicate that production companies achieve slightly better results than service companies but this difference is small.

Another category analyzed in detail was the dependence between customer acceptance towards a new product or service and the effectiveness of its diffusion. The obtained results made it possible to clearly evaluate the effectiveness of the innovation diffusion process implementation in the examined SMEs companies. The aggregated results have been presented in Table no. 4.

Table 4: Dependence of customer acceptance for implemented innovations and effectiveness of diffusion

Group	Category	Not	Some-times	Of-ten	Usual-ly	Al-ways
Services	Diffusion of innovation	31%	25%	23%	15%	6%
	Acceptance of customers	13%	14%	19%	25%	29%
Production	Diffusion of innovation	27%	26%	19%	17%	10%
	Acceptance of customers	18%	13%	14%	25%	30%
All	Diffusion of innovation	29%	26%	21%	16%	8%
	Acceptance of customers	16%	14%	16%	25%	29%

Source: own elaboration

As it seems from the obtained data, despite the fact that 29% of the introduced innovations always obtained customer acceptance, the diffusion of only 8% of them ended with a full market success. These results clearly indicate that the examined companies, in spite of the fact that they often have valuable, new products and services which obtain a positive customer evaluation, are very rarely able to carry out an effective process of their market diffusion. This is yet another confirmation of the thesis presented in the article that the examined companies have insufficient potential with regard to innovation diffusion. The detailed results providing the percentage share of profit on the sale of innovative products in the total profit of the researched companies are presented in Table no. 5.

Table 5: Average% share of profit from the sale of innovation

Size of the companies	Type of activity		Total Average
	Production	Service	
Small	9,8%	8,9%	9,35%
Micro	8,24%	6,49%	7,37%
Average	13,34%	12,78%	13,06%
Total Average	10,5%	9,39%	9,93%

Source: own elaboration

Due to the results obtained, the author has divided the surveyed companies into two groups:
- not innovative companies,
- innovative companies.

To the group of innovative companies, the author classified the company that in the first step of the analysis obtained 10% of the best average results.

Table 6: The results of clusters analysis

Type of business/ Stages of the innovation process.	Non innovative companies	Innovative companies
Culture of innovation and human resources development strategy	2,6	4,3
Internal communication within the company and its organization	2,0	4,3
Diffusion of innovation and commercialization	1,8	4
The issue of implementation of innovative	2,5	4,2
Financing of innovative projects	2,8	4,1
The issue of planning projects in the field of innovation	2,2	4,3
Problem of seeking ideas for innovation	2,4	4
Analysis of the situation and environment	2,8	4
Aggregate innovative potential	2,2	4,2
Numbers of companies in the group	165	35

Source: own elaboration

The data presented clearly indicate that innovative companies have a very low efficiency of of innovative activity. The effectiveness of innovation activities for companies with strong internal resources is much higher than for firms with low resources. Discussed difference is presented in Figure 1.

Figure 1: Relationship between the company's internal resources

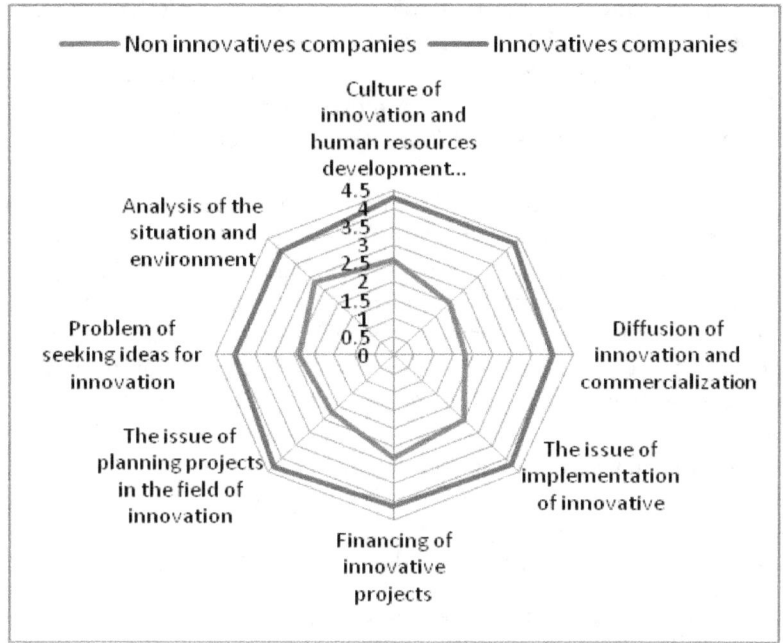

Source: own elaboration

The presented results seem to confirm the formulated thesis that there is the relationship between the company's internal resources and the effectiveness of innovative activity.

6 Summary, discussion and recommendations for further directions of researches on the efficiency of innovation activity of the SME companies

The author of this paper has formed a thesis that there is the relationship between the company's internal resources and the effectiveness of innovative activity. The presented results confirm the research hypothesis formulated by the author. Companies with low potential for innovation also showed very low efficiency in terms of innovation. This low potential in scope of the efficient implementation of diffusion processes is one (not the only – which is indicated by other, mentioned researches by the Author) of the determinants of the low innovation of Polish companies of the small and medium businesses sector. Despite the fact that 29% of the introduced innovations always obtained customer acceptance, the diffusion of only 8% of them ended with a full market success. As much as 54% of the examined companies declare that profits from the sale of innovations are below 10% of the total profit, and only 8% of the examined companies declare over 30% of profit from the sale of innovations. The obtained results should induce to conduct in-depth research in this respect. In-depth research, type case study would be significant from the point of view of evaluating the effectiveness of innovative processes. The diffusion processes of particular innovations should be subject to a detailed and thorough analysis as part of that research. Such research could help indicate specific mistakes made by companies when implementing diffusion processes. Research into the dynamics of changes of effectiveness of implementation of diffusion processes in time would also provide equally valuable information – this would enable drawing conclusions and evaluating whether SMEs are increasing their competencies in this aspect.

References

Angel H., Van de Ven A.H., 2000:Research on the management of innovation, Cambridge, MA: Ballinger.
Białoń, L. (Ed.), "Zarządzanie działalnością innowacyjną" [Managing innovation activities] (Placet, 2010)
Birchall, D.W., and Armstrong, M.S., Innovation Management: Achieving Multiple Objectives, (Henley Management College, 2001).
Bloch C., 2005: Innovation measurement: present and future challenges, Working paper from The Danish Centre for Studies in Research and Re-search Policy 2005/6.
Brzeziński M., (ed.) 2001: Zarządzanie innowacjami technicznymi i organizacyjnymi, Difin, Warszawa.
Cameron, K.S. and Quinn, R.E., "Kultura organizacyjna – diagnoza i zmiana. Model wartości konkurujących" [Diagnosing and Changing Organizational Culture: Based on the Competing Values Framework] (Oficyna Ekonomiczna, 2003).
Cooke, P. (Ed.), Handbook of Regional Innovation and Growth (Cheltenham: Edward Elgar Publishing Ltd., 2011).
Drucker P.F, 1994:Innovation and Entrepreneurship. Practice and Principles, Heinemann, London.
Fagerberg, J., "Innovation: A Guide to the Literature", In Fagerberg, J., Mowery, D.C., and Nelson, R.R. (Eds.)., The Oxford Handbook of Innovations (Oxford University Press, 2004).
Hall, B.H. and Rosenberg, N., Economics of Innovation (Elsevier, 2010).
Kanerva, M., Hollanders, H. and Arundel, A., Can We Measure and Compare Innovation in Services? (MERITMaastricht Economic Research Institute on Innovation and Technology, 2006).
Kaplan, R.S. and Norton, D.P., "Wdrażanie strategii dla osiągnięcia przewagi konkurencyjnej" [Implementation of Strategies to Achieve Competitive Advantage] (PWN, 2009).

Leading Issues in Innovation Research

Karganov S., 2008: Bariery obowiązującej teorii oceny efektywności ekonomicznej i drogi ich przezwyciężenia, in. „Tendencje innowacyjnego rozwoju polskich przedsiębiorstw". Instytut Wiedzy i innowacji, Warszawa, pp. 133-146.

Klein K.J, Sorra J.S.,1996: The challenge of innovation implementation. Academy of Management Review. v21 i4.

Klincewicz K., 2011: Dyfuzja innowacji. Jak odnieść sukces w komercjalizacji nowych produktów i usług, Wydawnictwo Naukowe Wydziału Zarządzania Uniwersytetu Warszawskiego, Warszawa.

Kline S.J., 1985: Innovation is not a Linear Process, Research Management, t. 28, 1985

Koberg, C.S., Detienne, D.R. and Heppard, K.A., "An Empirical Test of Environmental, Organizational and Process Factors Affecting Incremental and Radical Innovation", Journal of High Technolgy Management Research, Vol. 14, January 2003, pp. 21-45.

Lager, T., Managing Process Innovation: From Idea Generation to Implementation (Imperial College Press, 2011).

McKeown, M., The Truth About Innovation (Prentice Hall, 2008).

Miles, I., "Innovation in Services", In J. Fagerberg, D.C. Mowery, and R.R. Nelson (Eds.), The Oxford Handbook of Innovations (Oxford University Press, 2004).

Miller, D., "The Correlates of Entrepreneurship in Tree Types of Firms", Management Science, Vol. 29, No. 7, July 1983, pp. 770-791.

Norek T., 2011:Problems of SME Sector Enterprise Innovative Capacity Measurement in S. Hittmar (ed.) Theory of Management, The Selected Problems for the Development Support of Management Knowledge Base, University of Zilina, Zilina.

Norek T., 2012: The impact of the Innovative Potential of Polish SME Companies on their Innovative Activity Realization Models, GSTF Journal on Business Review (GBR - ISSN: 2010-4804), Vol 1 no. 4.

Norek T., 2013: Key barriers to the development of effective innovative activity of Polish SME companies. The relationship between the company's internal resources and the effectiveness of innovative activity. Business & Economics Society International, January 2013 Conference, Perth Australia

Norek, T., "Benchmarking innowacyjności przedsiębiorstw w regionie zachodniopomorski" [The Audit Platform as an Example of Benchmarking of Enterprise Innovation in West Pomerania Region], In Entrepreneurship, Innovation, Foresight: Aspects of Economic, Social and Ecological, L. Woźniak (Ed.; pp 273-282; Wydawnictwo Politechniki Rzeszowskiej, 2010).

Norek, T., "Problems of SME Sector Enterprise Innovative Capacity Measurement", In S. Hittmar (Ed.), Theory of Management: Selected Problems for the Development Support of Management Knowledge Base (University of Zilina, 2011).

Norek, T., "The Impact of the Innovative Potential of Polish SME Companies on their Innovative Activity Realization Models", GSTF Journal on Business Review, Vol. 1, No. 4, April 2012, pp. 77-84.

Okoń-Horodyńska, E. (Ed.), "Tendencje innowacyjnego rozwoju polskich przedsiębiorstw" [Tendencies in Innovative Development of Polish Enterprises] (Instytut Wledfzy i Innowacji, 2008).

Penrose, E. The Theory of the Growth of the Firm (John Wiley and Sons, 1959).

Podręcznik Oslo, 2005: Zasady gromadzenia i interpretacji danych dotyczacych innowacji, OECD i Eurostat.

Poznańska, K. "Uwarunkowania innowacji w małych i średnich przedsiębiorstwach", [Determinants of innovation in small and medium-sized enterprises]] (Dom Wydawniczy ABC, 1998)

Prahalad, C.K. and Krishnan, M.S., "Nowa era innowacji" [A New Era of Innovation] (PWN, 2010).
Pro Inno Europe, "Innovation Union Scoreboard 2010: Comparative Analysis of Innovation Performance", 2011a. Retrieved from http://www.proinno-europe.eu/innometrics/page/innovation-union-scoreboard-2010
Pro Inno Europe, "Summary Innovation Index", 2011b. Retrieved from http://www.proinno-europe.eu/page/summary-innovation-index-0#_ftn2
Rosebusch N., J. Brinckmann, A Bausch, 2009: Is New Better? A meta-Analysis of Innovation Performance Relationship in SME, American Academy of Management Conference, Chicago.
Rothwell R., 1994:Towards the Fifth Generation Process, International Marketing Review vol. 11 no.1.
Rothwell R., Zegveld W., 1985: Reindustrialisation and Technology, Longman, London.
Tidd, J., Bessant, J., and Pavitt, K., Managing Innovation: Integrating Technological, Market and Organisational Change (John Wiley & Sons Ltd., 2001).
Zahra, S.A., and Wiklund, J., "Top Management Team Characteristics and New Ventures' Product Innovation", paper presented at the American Academy of Management Conference, August 2010, Montreal.
Żołnierski, A., „Potencjał innowacyjny polskich małych i średniej wielkości przedsiębiorstw" [Innovation Potential of Polish SME Enterprises] (PARP, 2005).

www.ingramcontent.com/pod-product-compliance
Lightning Source LLC
Chambersburg PA
CBHW070335230426
43663CB00011B/2331